PSYCHOSIS RECOVERY GUIDE:

A Survivor's Handbook to Overcoming Mental Breakdown

by

Richard Forbes Steven

CONTENTS

DO YOU EXPERIENCE ANY OF THE FOLLOWING?

Thoughts that you do not normally have.
Thoughts that do not seem like your own.
Making unusual connections between people and things that you would not normally make.
Feeling like the Radio, TV, Internet, Phone, Social Media are all watching you and commenting on your behaviour personally.
Seeing 'signs' in various objects and experiences.
Hearing voices 'in your head'.
Seeing strange things.
Wanting to harm yourself.
Wanting to harm others.

Use your Voice - Ask for Help - It's OK - Call your Doctor!

If you are experiencing any of the above symptoms, make an appointment with your doctor now. Doctors are safe. Tell them everything that is going on, no matter how strange it seems. It may be that you are suffering from psychosis.

If you do not feel well enough to contact your doctor yourself, ask a friend, acquaintance or family member to help you and try to explain to them what you are experiencing. It can be scary to put these experiences into words, but you will feel better when you do. If your doctor gives you medication, take it! Follow your doctor's advice, it is important that you do this sooner rather than later because it is much easier to make a full recovery from psychosis if it is treated quickly. This is the first step in your recovery...

Authors Note: How To Use This Guide

Important: *The material in this guide is not a replacement for medical advice from your doctor and other healthcare professionals. I am not a doctor and I am not qualified to give medical advice. Always contact your doctor if you are feeling unwell and if you have any doubts or questions.*

The Psychosis Recovery Guide is meant as a support for your recovery alongside any other medical treatment that you receive. I suggest that you read through it once to get an overview of what it contains and then keep coming back to it and apply the methods as and when you need them, and when you feel like you have the capacity to use them. You can keep coming back again and again throughout all stages of your recovery. You will need to use some effort, but always remember to balance your effort with relaxation. It is important never to force anything.

Richard Forbes Steven

INTRODUCTION

I decided to write this Psychosis Recovery Guide because after the initial crisis stage of my own psychosis settled down, I discovered that there was a huge gap between the point where my medical treatment ended and my 'post-psychosis' life began. I lost a lot of time during the healing process, floundering around in the dark. If I had been introduced to a guide like this at the time, I am sure that I would have recovered much more quickly. So this work is an attempt to fill that gap and to offer useful insights that I hope will help facilitate your own swift recovery, or that of your friend or family member.

It has been an interesting and healing process for me to write this material because it feels like I am in fact writing a list of reminders to myself for my own continuing health and wellbeing. The process has reminded me of all of the things that I have done and still do for my own health, long after my psychosis has become a thing of the past.

Originally I thought that the guide would take the form of a 20-40 page help sheet, but I didn't realise until I started how much content there was. Now it has become a book! All of the tools in this guide have helped and worked for me at some point in my journey back to health and I am still coming back to them in one way or another myself. Not only are these tools useful for recovery from psychosis, but also for working with anxiety, depression, and for mental wellbeing in general, long after your psychosis has become a distant memory.

If these tools have worked for me, they can work for you too, or at least provide you with a map or starting point that can help you to find your own way. What they require is your engagement, participation and perseverance, even when you feel like it is all a big pointless waste of time. The rewards will come if you are active and take a positive interest in your own recovery.

In the first part of this guide, I share with you some of my own experiences with psychosis in order to give some insight into how the experience can be for someone who is in the middle of it. Of course, it is just one experience and it is very personal but I hope that some insights can be gained and some lessons can be learned that can inform your own recovery, or that of your friend or family member.

In the second part of this I guide, I lay out a set of practical steps that can be taken in order to help manage your condition. If you are a friend or family member, you can read this guide and use it to provide help and support your loved one. Be very careful to do this in a relaxed and gentle way without trying to push too hard or to be judgemental.

Depending on the cause, early identification and treatment of psychosis can provide a much higher probability of a full recovery. For this reason it is important to involve your doctor as soon as possible when symptoms start to appear and if possible try to 'catch' it before it goes too far. In any case, I sincerely hope that the material in this guide helps you by providing a set of principles, and practical tools to adopt, that will aid your swift recovery and help you to effectively manage your condition going forward.

WHAT IS PSYCHOSIS? AN EXPERIENTIAL POINT OF VIEW

Psychosis can be a terrifying condition, both for those who experience it and for friends and family. You will all find yourselves in uncharted waters if it is the first time that you have experienced this process, but it is good to know that there is a much higher recovery rate from psychosis when it is identified and treated early. For this reason, it is very important to be informed and aware about what this condition is and how to manage it. It is also useful to understand a little about what is going on for the person who is suffering from psychosis so that you can have some insight into some of the bewildering events that you may be experiencing or witnessing.

We all have unusual thoughts at times, it is a normal experience for everyone. Most people are able to understand that the strange thought that they are having is something without a basis in their reality. They can recognise the thought or thought process as unusual or strange and simply forget it, most of the time unconsciously or semi-consciously. These unusual thoughts and experiences are a little like some of the experiences we may have while dreaming except they happen when we are awake.

For a person who is beginning to suffer from psychosis, often in quite a gradual way, they will begin to give some credibility to their unusual thoughts and experiences and not be able to 'file them away' as strange or unusual. They will become real for that person. For example, you may be watching TV in your living room while thinking that you need to go outside and wash your car while the sun is shining. At that very same moment an advert comes onto the TV that says 'do you need to wash your car while the sun is shining?' For a moment we may think, 'Is the TV reading my mind?' and then brush it off as a ridiculous idea and forget about it almost instantly. A person who is beginning to suffer from psychosis may instead think that somehow the TV is reading their thoughts and commenting on them, which leads them towards a state of confusion, paranoia and anxiety.

This is a process that can happen in an increasing way over weeks, months and sometimes years. It can also happen rapidly depending on the circumstances of, and causes of the condition. Because of the sometimes gradual nature of onset, it can be difficult to identify that there is something wrong until the illness has become well developed both for the person suffering and for the people around them.

As this process continues, the person suffering may become increasingly introverted, antisocial, and paranoid. They may also 'act-out' and display unusual behaviours, along with compensating for their discomfort by self medicating with alcohol, drugs, sex and obsessive behaviours.

Over time, the shared consensus reality that most of us experience will no longer apply for that person. Their inherited frames of reference from family, friends and society begin to dissolve and are replaced by the 'dream-like' frames of reference that they begin to experience. The deeper they go into this state, the more consuming their new frames of reference will be until they are unable to distinguish 'dream' from consensus reality.

For the person experiencing psychosis, they literally experience a completely different dimension with its own rules that govern cause and effect and their experiences will become more and more extreme. They can start to hear voices, see 'signs' in material objects that have special 'significance' in the new world that they inhabit. They can misinterpret the things that people, friends and loved ones say (including TV, Radio, Music, Social Media etc). They may hear multiple meanings or even multiple voices speaking through the single person that they are talking to. These experiences can result in aggressive / passive aggressive behaviours if they feel threatened, but more likely, the person will become increasingly introverted. At this point, they may become totally alienated from family and friends and may engage in self harm or attempt suicide.

Unfortunately, for the person suffering from psychosis, their experiences will very often be persecutory and unpleasant and they will be suffering terribly. For this reason, it is really helpful to be able to 'catch' and treat the illness before it goes too far.

Because of the sometimes gradual onset of psychosis, it can be difficult for the person suffering, and also those around them to acknowledge that there is a problem. The strange experiences and behaviours can become somewhat normalised over time, until they become so extreme that they cannot be ignored. It is better not to let this happen and to intervene early if at all possible. That is where mental health education comes in, both on an individual level and also as a society, especially as the incidence of mental health conditions increases.

MY JOURNEYS INTO (AND OUT OF) PSYCHOSIS

I t may be useful for you to know about my personal experience with psychosis to give you some insight from a 'survivor's perspective' and to see what has led me to write this guide. In my case, the experience of full psychosis grew slowly over about three years leading to a crisis episode at the age of nineteen. It took me eight years and three hospitalisations to fully recover and the last 'episode' that I had was at the age of twenty seven.

The causes in my Case

There are many different causes of psychosis and psychosis is not considered to be a disease in itself but a collection of symptoms that can occur, usually as the result of a particular cause, or group of causes (long term stress, bereavement, schizophrenia, drug use, insomnia, genetics, trauma etc). In my case, the underlying causes were connected with my early family life and recreational drug use. Very simplistically, it went something like this.

A difficult set of family dynamics in my early life led to deep seated sense of insecurity and anxiety throughout my child-hood.

I developed a huge disrespect for authority and started play-ing-up at school and being disruptive in classes, looking for attention and validation.

I led a double life, behaving one way at home and one way at school and college. This dissonance was stressful and in the end, I couldn't be myself at home and I wasn't myself at school and college either. In fact, I had no idea who I was at all!

In order to cover up my feelings of anxiety, isolation and loneliness, I created a persona of being a 'rebel' at school, which made me quite popular, or at least well known.

As I entered my teens and my burgeoning sexuality started to develop, my insecurity and anxiety started to become more extreme.

I started to 'self medicate' by smoking cigarettes, using alco-hol and smoking cannabis, which on the one hand all seemed like great fun at the beginning, creating a feeling of tribe-like connection with my friends that was missing in other parts of my life, but on the other hand led to feelings of isolation from anyone who was outside of that 'scene'.

By the time I got to 6th Form college, we had all become fully fledged stoners, smoking dope full time, taking LSD, mush-rooms, amphetamines, cocaine etc. I dropped out in the sec-ond year of college to try to develop my interest in music.

After a while, things began to become increasingly fragmented. I became more and more isolated from my friends as we grew apart and I disappeared into an intoxicated haze while I ostensibly attempted to do something with my music with a local stoner who had a recording studio.

My anxiety increased and was such that I had to smoke a 16thoz of cannabis in order to be able to get to sleep. I became increasingly paranoid.

Gradual Onset of Psychosis

Paranoia

Paranoia was the first symptom of my slowly growing entry into the early symptoms of the psychotic state. I would think that my friends and family were talking about me behind my back, or thinking bad things about me. This is a feeling I had at various times throughout my childhood and into my teens.

Of course, this is normal. People talk about each other in positive and negative ways all the time, but because my underlying state was insecure and anxious, later fuelled by cannabis and other drugs (which induce paranoia), and hormones(!), I was hypersensitive, and began not to trust people at all. I had no stable base of self esteem to protect me.

If I had had some kind of 'paranoid' experience with someone, the next time I saw that person, my feeling towards them or behaviour would be a little different because I started to resent them for the things that I imagined that they were saying or thinking. This created a vicious circle of becoming more isolated and at the same time suspicious towards my friends and family. I started surrounding myself with people who were much older than me in order to provide myself with a sense of self importance to cover for my insecurity. These people were not so connected to my immediate circle and were also deeper into the 'drug scene', so I felt like I was being a badass, though, as a result, I became more and more isolated.

When my symptoms progressed, my paranoia began to extend to a larger scale where I began to feel like I was being watched, and also that my thoughts were affecting world events. For example, I remember one day having some angry thoughts, and then reading in a newspaper about a natural disaster that had happened in a far away country where many people had died. I felt like I had been responsible for that disaster because I connected it with the angry thoughts that I had, and understood that the reporting in the newspaper was referring to me as the cause.

When I fell in love with a friend's younger sister when I was 19 years old, things began to fragment even more. Falling in love was an experience that I had absolutely no emotional tools to deal with and amplified my feelings of paranoia, insecurity and anxiety to an extreme that I was simply not able to handle.

Magical Thinking And Delusion

I suppose that it is a natural step for someone who is suffering from quite extreme low self esteem, insecurity and anxiety to ask themselves 'What is this all about?', 'Why am I suffering so much?', 'Why are we here?'. At the same time, smoking cannabis and experimenting with psychedelics can give one the illusion of insight into some of these areas and bring out the more philosophical aspects of life. During my teens, in order to try to find some answers to these questions, I became fascinated by mysticism, shamanism and transcendent wisdom traditions. Particularly the books of Carlos Castaneda and books about Tibetan Buddhism.

'Magical thinking' and 'delusional thinking' are characteristic of psychosis and the mystical books that I was reading fed into the internal mythology that was gradually growing inside me. I began to experience very literally some of the things that I had read about.

The point here is that the mind is extremely powerful, and when unbalanced, the things that we expose ourselves to can become the fuel for the psychotic reality that we create. It will be different for everyone who goes through psychosis. If someone reads a lot of comic books for example, it is quite possible that their psychosis experience may refer to the life depicted in the comic book and become real for them. For me, I began to identify with the experiences of Carlos Castaneda and the various Yogi's in the books on Tibetan Buddhism that I read along with other things related with my subconscious, circumstances, family and friends.

Hearing Voices

The next phase that developed for me was hearing voices. Remembering it now, as it began, it seems like it was an externalisation of my paranoia. I was experiencing my paranoia in the form of male and female voices who were 'observing' me. At first, I might hear just a little giggle, or some murmurs in response to something that I might have thought or done. It might be something I heard in my head, or it may also be a combination of sounds such as the sound of wind blowing in the trees that I would misinterpret as voices. At the time, I thought 'well it's just because I am stoned'. Later these voices developed more and more and became particularly strong during the first time that I had sex, where several female voices that seemed to me like a group of witches said 'now we've got him!'. The voices were also much stronger when I was alone, and at night time.

My First Full Blown Crisis

My first full blown psychotic crisis happened when I was 19 years old and was a terrifying experience.

I was sitting in a music session at a local music producers recording studio. These sessions usually involved smoking copious amounts of cannabis and taking other recreational drugs. Even before I arrived at the studio, I felt extremely nervous and paranoid. The people there were not really my friends and they were much older than me, but I wanted to be around them because I was interested in making music and I wanted to try to learn from them. They were also into 'psychedelic shamanism' which was fascinating for me, as well as scary, and by then, I had started to project all sorts of magical qualities onto them that I had drawn from reading Carlos Castaneda and other books. I imagined them performing all sorts of magical rituals, having wild orgies and travelling between the worlds.

At a certain point, not really knowing what exactly we were smoking, time seemed to slow down. I looked at the person next to me and they appeared to be moving, in both slow motion and fast-forward motion simultaneously.

I began to feel like what was happening was some kind of initiation. Nothing was said, but I felt that all my ancestors and all my family and all the people that I had ever had a connection with in my life were waiting in the field above the studio for me to find the courage to go to join them. If I did this, I would be welcomed back into the tribe as a fully initiated member. I felt torn between my immense fear of the craziness of this experience and the wish to rejoin my 'tribe' and be accepted. As I sat there, the pressure began to mount. There was an imperative building and only a small window of time in which I could join the 'tribe'. If I missed this window, I would be 'hunted'.

Eventually, I could not stand the fear and pressure and stood up suddenly saying that I was leaving. I never went to the field above the studio to meet 'the tribe' but went to my car and drove away, terrified, all the time hearing voices saying that I had run away and that I should be ashamed and that now they will have to hunt me down.

As I drove, I saw headlights behind me and thought that someone had been sent to run me off the road. I took quite a long detour in order to be able to lose this car and then went home to my parents house and walked in to their bedroom to check if they were there, as I thought that they had been in the field above the studio. Of course they were in bed and were a little surprised that I had entered their room, but in the back of my disturbed mind, I thought that they were pretending and that in fact they had rushed back to the house from the farm where the studio was. I went into my own bedroom, sat on my bed and had the vertiginous sense that I had dreamed the whole thing.

The next day, I woke up and felt like I had died and was in some kind or after-death state. At the same time, I felt such a strong feeling of guilt and shame that I had 'failed the test'.

My parents at this time were physically present but they seemed like shells to me, as did everyone else. I felt that they were all associated with one kind of faction or other and that because I had not completed my initiation, I was in no-mans-land and fair game for attack from all sides. At this point I experienced symbolic death over and over again. I heard funeral music in the village and thought that people were enacting my funeral.

I began seeing signs and connections between everything, the shapes of clouds, the shapes in rocks, symbols in trees, symbols in speech. I felt particularly connected to crows, ravens, buzzards and seagulls, each of which had their own tribe that connected with and dominated the human world. I thought that everyone else could interpret these signs and could communicate telepathically with each other but because I had not gone through to the end of the 'initiation', I had no full access to this network. I also started to feel that the television, newspapers, radio and music were directing their attention towards me and commenting on my thoughts and actions. I remained in this unbalanced state for the next year to one degree or another.

Things get somewhat fuzzy at this point in terms of how I managed this situation, but I was not treated immediately. At that time (late 1990's), there wasn't the same level of social awareness about mental health as there is now and there was also a much greater taboo about mental health, especially in rural areas like Cornwall where I grew up. So as far as I can tell, the people around me mostly tried to ignore it and hoped that it would go away.

I remember going to the doctor at one point but he didn't seem to take what I was telling him very seriously. I was also so caught up in my delusional reality that it meant that I thought the doctors were all 'in on it'!

Meeting my Teacher, Namkhai Norbu Rinpoche

In November 1994, while in this unstable state, I went with some friends to a retreat with a Tibetan spiritual master called Namkhai Norbu Rinpoche.

I had been reading books about meditation and Tibetan Buddhism, and my friend's mother invited me to come because she knew that I was interested in it. I knew that things were not right with me and at that point thought that I would try anything to help my situation, so I went along.

I didn't know anything about the teacher or the 'Dzogchen Atiyoga' teachings that he was giving. On the journey to the retreat I saw several crows flying with us along with the car as if they were escorting us. In fact, I had the sense that we were not really driving to the place at all but that we were magically taking flight through some kind of multidimensional space, guided by the crows. As I mentioned before, the 'Crow Tribe' played a big role in my symbolic world and it felt like there were powerful forces at play.

When we arrived at the retreat, it was in a wet field in Wales, we were all camping in tents and the teachings themselves were being held in a huge mongolian style Yurt, which seemed very exotic to me. I felt totally neurotic and found it very difficult to connect with any of the people there, although many of them were later to become part of a large extended family.

On the first day of the teaching, we went into the Yurt in which there were around 200 people. In front of us, there was a raised platform with several Tibetan Thangkas (paintings) and a seat for the teacher. It was quite overwhelming for me to be around so many people in a confined space. I remember being so nervous that I kept having to go to outside to pee.

We sat there and waited for what seemed like a long time and at a certain point everyone began to stand up. After a while I heard a deep, jolly, resonant voice greeting people and laughing. Rinpoche entered the tent and walked to his seat in front of us. He was not a tall man but was solid and strong, and as he walked inside, the sound of his footsteps seemed to boom through the tent. I had an indescribable sensation that I knew him already, which was absolutely electric. He had a huge presence for me and for the first time in a long time, I felt some relief. I just knew immediately that even though my world had totally fallen apart that if I followed what this man taught, everything would be OK.

Looking back on it, I can see that I was extremely fortunate that Namkhai Norbu Rinpoche was an authentic teacher because many people in similar vulnerable states may well meet unqualified people who would take advantage of them. In the Tibetan tradition, it is recommended that one spends seven years assessing the authenticity of a teacher before deciding to follow them. I do not recommend throwing yourself into a spiritual tradition in the way that I did without checking it out thoroughly first. This is the beauty of hindsight. In any case, I was fortunate!

Over the next five days we received Dzogchen teachings about the nature of the mind. It was difficult for me to understand the individual words that were being taught because I was unwell and there were also certain terms and concepts that were very unfamiliar to me. On a fundamental level though, intuitively, I felt that I understood perfectly that what was being communicated was a state, and did not depend at all on the words that were being said but depended totally on the connection one has with the teacher and one's ability to be receptive.

The word Dzogchen itself means 'Self Perfection' and the Dzogchen teachings are a series of methods and instructions that introduce students to the recognition of the nature of Mind. This is the state of naked awareness totally beyond thoughts and concepts. Dzogchen practitioners will develop and expand their recognition of this state through practice until it eventually embraces and integrates everything that they perceive and do. This state of recognition and integration of the nature of Mind is considered to be freedom and liberation from suffering and its root, which is dualistic vision.

My friend and I would literally run to the tent in the morning to get to the teaching session, full of excitement. When Rinpoche was teaching it felt like he looked at me many times and that the recognition that I felt was completely mutual and that he was very happy to see me. Of course this was probably a delusion, but it felt extremely special at the time!

The teachings themselves were perfect for me and completely satisfied my thirsty mind. Namkhai Norbu Rinpoche was an astonishing teacher. One of the most striking things for me was his absolute confidence and mastery over his subject. It was obvious that he was not just teaching abstract concepts, but knowledge that he actually inhabited through his direct experience.

The teachings that we received were related with the transference of consciousness at the time of death and dying (*Phowa*), a topic that was very immediate for me at that time (when I wasn't always sure if I was alive or not). There was a kind of elemental drama too. Rinpoche would be transmitting various Mantras or we would be doing practices together as a group and the wind would be blowing with the huge tent flapping strongly and rain drumming down deafeningly as if all the forces of nature were collaborating with the event. There were times that I was literally shaking with the power of it.

Going to this retreat in fact became the most important event in my life, as it provided me with many of the tools that I needed in order to eventually be able to overcome my psychosis and to be able to write this guide!

Some Respite

At some point I was prescribed a medication called Stelazine (trifluoperazine hydrochloride), but it did not suit me very well and gave me many unpleasant side effects like dizziness and lethargy. Later, when it was clear that the medication wasn't working for me, my parents took me to a private hospital in Exeter where I was prescribed a drug called Sulpiride that did suit me better and it began to stabilise my condition. At no point that I was aware of did I receive any formal diagnosis or explanation of what was going on. I was given the pills and no other care or support was offered by the medics.

For the following two or so years, I would say that I remained in a borderline state where I was living partially in a delusional world and partially in regular society. I was a 'semi-functional psychotic'. When I was doing so called 'normal' things, the paranoia and anxiety were always present, as were the symbolic connections I was seeing in everything along with the tribal spirit-world delusions.

I continued taking medication and I started to make some positive steps in the sense that I began to avoid all of the friends that I had who were smoking dope. I also began to do some voluntary work in a local holiday centre for disabled people which helped to some extent to build my confidence, surrounded by people who were not connected to my past. I started to do the meditation practices that I had learned at the retreat with Namkhai

Norbu Rinpoche every day, with the help of a recording that I had, and I felt that this helped a lot.

Eventually I felt strong enough to move to Cheltenham where I lived in a bedsit for about a year near my brother who had been at university there. I felt like I had to get away from my environment and also the people I knew, all of which, and whom seemed to be reinforcing my illness through negative association and habit.

I started to feel better and better and did more voluntary work for an organisation called the Winged Fellowship Trust (now called Revitalise). This was convenient because it was residential and I could go and work for two weeks and then come home for two weeks and then go to work again. It was a really good way to do something useful, gain some confidence and work experience, increase my social skills and meet nice people. I made some good friends at that time and there were moments where I felt content and happy, although I was always a little 'on the edge' and was continuing to take a reduced dose of medication. I also managed to have some intimate, sexual friendships with girls which was something that I had struggled with before, although it would be years before I was able to have actual relationships.

Later, I went to Scotland and hitch hiked around the highlands with a friend that I met while doing voluntary work with the Winged Fellowship Trust. Things were looking up and I seemed to be doing things that 'normal' people in their early twenties might do!

My Second Crisis

At the end of my trip to Scotland, I went to Samye Ling Tibetan Buddhist centre in Dumfriesshire. I guess I was drawn there by my interest in Tibetan Buddhism and the mystical side of life, and also through the positive experience that I had with Namkhai Norbu Rinpoche. I felt that I needed some more personal guidance from some qualified teachers.

I stayed in Samye Ling for about four months. The first two months were great, but at a certain point I started to fall apart. Probably at this point, I had stopped taking my medication, thinking that the power of the 'Yogic' practices that I was doing could overcome any problems. Not a good idea at that point!

Apart from not taking my medication, there was something about being in the environment at Samye Ling that made my paranoia and insecurity return. There was something about the mysticism and exoticness of it along with an institutional and spiritually aspirational atmosphere there that seemed some-how stressful and didn't sit very well with me. I think also that the rich symbolism of the Tibetan monastic environment strongly triggered and fed into the magical world that I had cre-ated for myself during my earlier episodes.

I started to hear voices again and have strange experiences, this time on a much more extreme level. I did not just hear a few voices but whole 'stadiums' full of thousands of voices all joined together in unison. At times, I felt like the symbolic object of a spirit-world game with competing sides battling for possession of my consciousness. My thoughts, feelings and actions were all on display down to the most minute detail and would be as-sessed and analysed. Based on this analysis, there would be con-sequences, sometimes good in the form of blissful sensations and sometimes in the form of punishments like the experience of a cold hell. The crowds of voices would roar and cheer, or boo and taunt me depending on what was going on. It was abso-lutely exhausting and terrifying.

At one point, I thought that maybe if I became a monk, I might be protected from attack. I didn't really want to be a monk because deep down, if I only had the confidence, I wanted to have lots of sex with as many different women as possible at that point! But it seemed like the spiritual power of monk-hood would help me, so I went through with it and became ordained.

Unfortunately it didn't help, and things only became worse. I lasted a month as a monk before I handed back my robes and left, hitch-hiking to see my brother and friend Tanya in Edinburgh.

When I got to Edinburgh, I was not in a good state at all. I began to have suicidal thoughts about jumping out of my brother's apartment window which was 6 floors or so up. I was experiencing strong sensations of persecution coupled with huge shame. At this moment though, the 'voices' actually saved me to some extent because they said 'you know what will happen if you do that...' then I heard some computer-game-like sound effects and there was a kind of demonstration. It became clear that if I jumped out of the window, it would not be 'over' at all so I stayed put.

After a day or two, my brother walked with me to the psychiatric hospital in Edinburgh and I checked in. I was only there for a short time when some friends from Samye Ling came to take me away again, I am not sure what they were thinking...

Eventually, I went back to Cornwall on the train and stayed at my parents house for a few days and after it became clear to them that I was not well at all, my Mum encouraged me to get some help and I was admitted to hospital voluntarily. This time for a full month.

The Hospital Experience

All hospitals are different and I think that the experience one can have will depend very much on where you are and how well organised and funded the local healthcare services are. I think that I was fortunate in that the hospital I went to was in a quiet, rural location and was well established. I also think that it was a good thing that I was a voluntary patient, as to have been admitted to hospital as a result of a section would have added layers of stress and complication to a situation that was already complicated enough.

Arrival

I don't remember much about arriving at the hospital itself, only some fleeting memories of the reception area before I was shown to a small room which was to be mine for several days. It was simple and comfortable.

On the first night, the hallucinations that I was experiencing were very strong and involved epic tribal battles between the vying factions of powerful forces who were attempting to dominate me. Every sound in the hospital seemed connected to my inner experience of this struggle, along with all of the noises outside my window. At times the sounds would join together in unison to become one huge voice that would shout at me saying something like 'you need to choose who to join!'. Now, along with the elusive Crow Tribe, there were Christians (a faction that seemed to have a strong hold in Cornwall), Corn Magic (another, older, Pagan faction connected with Cornwall) and Buddhists. There were also the Seagulls who were beings only concerned with fulfilling their gluttonous instincts, and then there were the normal humans.

In time, it became clear that I was not going to join anything and at that moment because I had a strong sense that if I became part of any one thing that it would become a limitation, so all of the factions turned on me. 'You have lost your honour, now you have no choice but to kill yourself'. I looked out of the window and saw a small sliver of glass that looked like it had been placed specifically to encourage me to cut my wrists with. All the signs were saying 'it's over, you have no other choice'. I tried to do some of the meditation practices that I had learned to protect myself from this attack but it only seemed to inflame the situation.

I laid down on my bed, and outside my door, I could hear a care support staff member standing and waiting. I am sure that I heard him say 'well if you don't do it, I am going to come in there and do it for you!'. He was probably there in fact on suicide watch. I sat up on my bed, dazed and spinning while I contemplated taking my own life. In that moment, I remembered a book that I had read by H.H. Dalai Lama where he said that what happens after you die depends very much on the state you are in when you die and has a strong influence on the kind of vision you will enter after death. At that point I had a jarring insight into what would happen if I dropped my body at that point. I knew that I was not in a good state, and what I saw was terrifying. It didn't look like there was any coming back from that awful state and that to some extent, my physical body was something like a safety ring that gets thrown to someone who is drowning at sea. It was the only thing that was keeping me afloat from entering much lower states of consciousness and suffering.

After seeing this after-death state, it became crystal clear to me that at the very least, I was not going to take my own life. I had found the floor. The only way was up from here. I became indignant, defiant. 'Come and do it then if you have to but I won't. No way' I thought to myself about the man outside my door. Then I just lay on my bed and spent a long time repeating to myself over and over again, sometimes out loud 'everything will be ok, everything will be ok, everything will be ok.' 'I am going to live a positive, happy and fulfilling life, I am going to live a positive, happy and fulfilling life.' I put everything into these phrases, and others, all my intention and emotion until a part of me gradually started to wake up and begin to believe that these things may be possible, something like a shoot, growing from a seed. At some point I went to sleep.

A Bad Reaction

At the beginning of my stay in hospital, I was given a drug that did not suit me at all. It may have been Stelazine once again. Perhaps it was the drug of choice at that time. In any case the side effects for me were very unpleasant. My tongue became enlarged and quite stiff, making it difficult to speak properly. It was upsetting to experience. As well as this, I started to become very dizzy and unstable on my feet and almost couldn't walk up the corridor of the hospital without holding onto the wall. At a certain point I just broke down crying and had to explain what was going on to the nursing staff. I also told them that I had used another drug called Sulpiride which had worked well for me in the past. Fortunately, the doctors took this on board and changed my medication over to Sulpiride and thankfully things began to improve.

Hospital Routine

After about a week, my symptoms slowly began to calm down to a more manageable level and I started to settle down into the routine of being in hospital without feeling so paralysed by my hallucinatory world.

The routine mostly rotated around meal times and medication distribution. We would have breakfast at around 8am which would be followed by medication, which we would queue up at a trolley to receive from a nurse. Then, we were free to do what we wanted. There was a TV room, a games room for quiet games like scrabble and other board games and another that housed a pool table, the dining area, the general ward sleeping area which had a typical hospital bed setup with beds surrounded by curtains and some individual rooms where new arrivals were housed. There was also a small outside area which had a garden. At the beginning, I mostly rested and slept. I was exhausted and didn't have any energy to do anything.

There was a lot of sitting around smoking. At this time in the 1990's there was no smoking ban for indoor spaces in the way that there is now, so many people were just sitting around, watching TV and smoking, including me! It seems strange to think of it now.

Visitors were quite free to come and go throughout the day, perhaps because it was a voluntary ward and had more relaxed rules about this than a section ward. My mum came quite often to visit and we would play games like Scrabble (which I hate, but it was nice to have some human contact).

Other Patients

At the beginning of my stay in hospital, I was slightly nervous about some of the other people I would meet there. My stereotype of a mental hospital was that it would be a dangerous place full of crazy psychopaths. What I found mostly were people just like me. People who for one reason or another simply couldn't cope with life at that moment in time and who seriously needed some time-out to rest and get themselves back together. These were vulnerable people and I became fond of some of them. We were all connected by our vulnerability. It is true, there were some colourful characters in there but I didn't feel threatened by anyone. There was also no judgement, which was liberating. There was an unspoken sense of camaraderie and acceptance between us. It didn't matter what anyone did or said.

I made a couple of friends who I would play pool or go for walks with. I actually became quite good at pool in the hospital and I began to be able to laugh for the first time in a long time. There were others who I would have conversations with, and we would talk about our lives and what had brought us to the hospital and the kinds of things we might like to do once we leave. It felt good to connect with other patients there. It was humanising to feel that I was not alone and that other people had similar stories and experiences.

Talking Therapy

Apart from my symptoms subsiding as a result of taking medication, the most useful therapeutic intervention that I received in hospital was a counselling session with one of the counselling staff. Unfortunately, I only had one session but it felt really good to be able to just say what was on my mind to someone who was neutral and only there to listen. I felt a lot better afterwards and it gave me confidence that counselling is a useful form of therapy. I would recommend anyone who is going through psychosis either in hospital or at home to seek counselling and continue with it long term. I did not have the possibility to do it at that time, but a lot later I did, and I still make use of it today. It is partly as a result of the counselling that I have received that I have been able to finally write this guide.

Getting Ready to Leave

After the third week in hospital, I had started to feel much better. I had come back to earth and the symptoms of my psychosis had faded into the background. I was starting to feel that I didn't need to be there any more and my energy was returning somewhat although I still felt tired and spaced-out. I have to say that I felt a great sense of gratitude that the medication had worked for me and that my stay in hospital had provided a safe space in which I could recover. It was such a relief.

Now, I was challenged with the question, what next? How do I come back from this? While I felt much better in terms of my symptoms of psychosis, I was going back into the world after having fallen apart completely. I had no idea what I was doing. All I knew was that I would go back to stay at my parents' house, which was not really the best place for me to be for many different reasons.

Finally the day came when I was to leave hospital. I remember my mother and my brother being there. I felt a mixture of excitement mixed with trepidation and humiliation. There is a certain kind of shame that I felt to have had such a mental health crisis that it took me years to get over. There was also a huge fear of slipping back down into it. I hope that for people suffering from psychosis and other mental health crises today that they are much better informed than I was at that time.

Convalescence

I wasn't at my parents house for too long before I reconnected with an old school friend who had just returned from a sailing expedition in the Canary islands and who was also wondering what to do with himself. He had previously lived in Falmouth in Cornwall and was thinking of moving back down there. We decided to move down together and share a flat. I was a little surprised that he would be open to doing this considering what I had been through. Again, I was unnecessarily projecting the shame and stigma of having had a mental health problem onto my friend. Thankfully he was a very kind person, open and non-judgemental.

After a short time, I had started a new life in Falmouth. I wasn't working and entered an arty, bohemian scene that suited me really well at the time. I felt more or less comfortable sur-rounded by creative people, students and oddballs. Falmouth was full of all of them and there was a great social scene that revolved around music, art and parties. I would drink alcohol with my friends, but my days of smoking cannabis and taking other drugs were completely over. Sometimes I felt excluded because all of my friends were doing these things, but there was just no way.

At the beginning, my life in Falmouth just consisted of 'hanging out'. I started a small music project which was rewarding and made many new friends. I had a lot of fun and it all seemed quite idyllic. It was just what I needed and was more or less all I felt I could cope with. It was like living a student life without being a student.

I ended up moving around a lot in Falmouth and hanging out with different people. Looking back on it, I can see that I had absolutely no idea what I was doing. I was drifting about with no direction and receiving state benefits. I had no idea of the future and felt so affected by my experience with psychosis that I didn't even consider that I might have some kind of future other than the one I was living at that time. I had no dreams, no ambition and no goals. In a way, I felt quite free, it was all very idyllic, although I still felt anxious and neurotic, but many of the people I was around at the time had similar problems so it felt somehow okay.

Third Crisis & Hospitalisation

At a certain point, I began once again to descend into the psychotic state. It is difficult for me to remember what the triggers for this may have been and also the exact timeline of events, but I began again to enter into my symbolic world in a much more intense way than before.

This time, the experience started with increasing levels of anxiety which led to quite extreme insomnia. As this developed, I became more and more fragile and stopped being able to filter 'strange' thoughts out from 'normal' ones. I lost my appetite and lost quite a lot of weight. I again entered fully into the 'other' place and had several strong experiences.

At one point, a voice said to me 'Richard, you need to lie down, we are going to re-pattern you.' I lay down on my bed and was attended to by what seemed like hundreds of beings who rapidly unravelled me, as if my whole being was like a ball of string made of light and mental formations that was coded with different experiences and 'patterns' that determined who I was and the kind of vision and experiences of the world that I would have. This coded pattern went back into the whole of evolutionary history. I could almost sense my ancestors along with all the people and experiences that had shaped my current life. After I had experienced this unravelling process completely which related mainly with the past until the present, I was 'repatterned'. New strands and threads were woven together in order to re-make me and this related to how my life would unfold from now on into the future. I could see all of this information entering my 'strands' and also had some influence over some things that I could add. There was a theme about evolution, of achieving enlightenment, of going beyond limitations, but there was huge danger involved too of encoding things that would then become obstacles and limitations in the future.

I have no idea where the re-patterning theme came from, but other more familiar themes emerged such as going through a symbolic death repeatedly and many other experiences similar to those that I have mentioned above.

Eventually, an acquaintance of mine, Richard found me sitting on a bench in the middle of Falmouth. It was difficult for me to speak because of the intensity of what I was experiencing internally. I was mostly staring into space, overwhelmed. He understood that there was something wrong and said 'don't you think it would be a good idea to see a doctor and get some help?' 'You don't seem very well.' I was in a terrible state and I had to agree with him. He walked me home and we sat in my living room while they called the doctor. Soon, we saw my doctor and they drove me to the hospital in Truro where I stayed, this time for five days. Fortunately, even though my symptoms were much more intense, my recovery was much quicker than before.

I don't remember too much about this third stay in hospital. It was though, the first time that I had received an actual diagnosis that I knew about. I found out what my diagnosis was only because I could see what the doctor had written in his notes. Again, I do not remember anything being communicated to me about what psychosis is, but I do remember that I wasn't diagnosed with schizophrenia because I still had insight into my condition. I was able to sit and relate what I was experiencing to the doctor. I had this capacity if I was inhabiting a given frame of reference such as a doctors office.

Apart from these things, the only memories that I have from this stay in hospital are that the place near my bed smelled of urine and that at that point my meditation practice was much more developed and I was able to sit and meditate on my bed. I was also much more familiar with the hospital experience than I had been previously and knew what to expect, which perhaps allowed me to enter into the 'recovered' state more rapidly.

Getting Functional

There came a time during my stay in Falmouth that I began to realise that I cannot just drift about there forever. I needed to be proactive in healing myself and also in getting some confidence back and being functional in the world. I took several steps in order to do this.

Volunteering

It became clear to me that at some point I needed to work, but that I was actually unemployable, partly because I had no confidence and also because I had no particular skills. It seemed like one of the best ways, once again, to gain skills and confidence was to do voluntary work.

One day in Falmouth, I went to a 'Green Fair' in the local school where the British Trust for Conservation Volunteers (BTCV) also had an office. I met with some of the people that worked there and signed up to go along regularly to work with them. At that point I was still a little fragile, but it was good for me to go and do physical work and to be around people. It is the kind of work that gets one outside into nature and is practical and satisfying. At times it could be very funny too depending on the combination of characters that went along.

Mostly, our work consisted of clearing footpaths and planting trees in the Cornish countryside and planting Marram Grass in the sand dunes by the sea. It was the kind of work where you could just grab some tools and get on with it. If you wanted to talk to people, you could talk. If not, it didn't matter. Volunteering became a very useful stepping stone in order to gain confidence, social skills and future paid work.

My First Jobs

After working with the BTCV for some time, I got a part time job working with the Devon and Cornwall Autistic Community Trust. I had a friend who was working for them and after talking to him, it sounded like the kind of work that I might be able to do as it also connected with my earlier experiences of volunteering with care work.

It was a little ironic that I was doing care work with autistic people but I felt like I was borderline between being the carer and needing to be cared for! In any case it was very rewarding and I worked there for more or less one year doing personal care, cooking and taking groups of clients out on day trips. After a year of this work, I moved on as I found that some aspects of the job were not suitable for me, particularly dealing with very violent clients who would 'kick off' quite regularly which I found difficult to handle.

The next job I had was in a high-end restaurant as a waiter in Mylor Harbour near Falmouth which again was good experience and helped me to gain some confidence in a regular job. After a while I became the head waiter there and was tasked with training the new employees that were taken on. It was rewarding in some ways, although my boss was an unpleasant 'petty tyrant' type which became wearing.

Some time later, I had a job in a local recycling startup that was pretty basic work, driving around different pickup routes to houses and restaurants of people who wanted to recycle their waste and also sorting out the rubbish in the warehouse and taking it to the recycling centre for weighing. It was dirty, messy work, and the pay was terrible but I quite enjoyed the pure physicality and simplicity of it and we always listened to great music on the stereo in the warehouse. I enjoyed the feeling of being completely tired in a physical way at the end of the day. I think that I never had problems sleeping while I was doing that job!

The Barn

One of the steps I took in order to get back on my feet was to go to a place called 'The Barn' in Totnes, Devon, where I spent seven months. It seems amazing now after having lived in various countries around the world and also cities like London, but I remember leaving Cornwall on the train at that time, saying goodbye to my parents who came to see me off and going to Totnes and feeling literally terrified. It was nerve-wracking to leave the safety of my familiar environment in Falmouth and go out into the world. The world in this case being Totnes which is a small town in the countryside about an hour away!

The Barn was a rural retreat centre where people can practice meditation and Yoga while living in a conscious community environment. There were meditation sessions three times per day, some of which were guided by a selection of different instructors such as Stephen and Martine Batchelor and other experienced meditators. We also worked on the land growing vegetables and managing woodland. Once a week, we would have a 'talking stick' session where everyone in the group would be given the opportunity to express themselves without interruption about their experiences and personal processes in the place. This was a wonderful opportunity to learn about communication, trust and how to develop wisdom in a community environment.

I went to The Barn because I thought that it would be a safe place to start to enter into society while developing my interest in and practice of meditation and also to gain strength in order to manage my mental health. It was a very positive experience for me and helped me to continue to develop my set of internal tools that would eventually enable me to manage my mental health effectively.

'Try to do Something Concrete with your Life'

In November 1998, I met my teacher Namkhai Norbu Rinpoche for the second time at a retreat that he gave in Wales. It was amazing to see him again as I had been practicing as much as possible according to my capacity. I had also begun connecting with other practitioners in the Dzogchen Community who were his students and learning from them. My understanding and experience of the teaching and practice was gradually deepening.

At one point during this retreat I went to him and told him that I had been having problems with my mental health and hearing voices along with other strong experiences. It was an interesting moment. Rinpoche looked at me very sharply and I felt like the hall we were in had disappeared and that we had arrived somewhere else but somehow our minds were unified. Rinpoche then said 'yes' which seemed to communicate 'yes, that's it, that is the correct state'. Then everything came back and Rinpoche simply said 'try to do something concrete with your life'.

After that moment, the words 'try to do something concrete with your life' became a kind of riddle for me. What did that mean? It is still something that I consider today and it was good advice and can be applied on many different levels. It is probably one of the main reasons that I have written this guide! At that time, when I went back to Falmouth, I thought about this advice a lot and came to the conclusion that I could apply it on the one hand to the development of my meditation and spiritual practice and on the other hand by gaining some kind of qualification that allows me to do something useful in a concrete way. I decided that I would go to university and do a degree, because that is what people do in order to get on in life.

Getting into University

After having decided to go to university, I went to the local library and looked at the UCAS book which was the volume that listed all universities and their courses in the UK for a particular year. I had no particular idea about money or a career path at that point. I simply looked through the book and tried to find something that interested me.

The course that looked the most interesting was a BSc (Hons) in Traditional Chinese Medicine. I wanted to do something useful and Traditional Chinese Medicine was interesting to me as it was connected to Chinese philosophy and other things like Qigong and meditation, all of which I was interested in. On the other hand, as a science degree, there were many aspects of Western medicine that were included which were also very interesting. Mostly though, I thought that I would learn things that may help me to manage my mental health.

It was a 5 year course and involved spending 6 months studying in Beijing, the idea of which was nerve wracking, but I thought that by the end of five years, it probably wouldn't be a problem. The main part of the course though was in London, and at that time, I just didn't think that I could cope with living in such a huge city. The idea terrified me. For that reason, I gave up on the idea of doing that particular course and chose another that was a Western Herbal Medicine degree in the countryside near Eastbourne. I could much better visualise myself in some nice country environment quietly learning about herbs!

The next 'concrete' step that I needed to take was to gain some qualifications that would allow me to enter a university degree as I had no A-Levels since dropping out of college. Fortunately, there were A-Level equivalent access courses on offer in Biology and Chemistry which I could complete in one year as a distance-learning student. I decided to go for it!

The access courses were very challenging, especially the Chemistry. I have never felt very comfortable with maths, and working with chemical equations was a total nightmare. Fortunately I had a friend, Athene, who was excellent with chemistry and was kind enough to help me understand what I was doing. It seemed easy for her, which I found unfathomable! In any case, I was finally able to pass the access course exams with A grades and I was accepted onto the degree course.

By the end of the summer in 2000 I had moved to Eastbourne where my course was located and I lodged with a nice family there. Then, three days before the course was supposed to start, I was informed that it had been cancelled! What was I supposed to do? I had already moved!

I decided that since I had already uprooted myself, I may as well go all the way and try to attend the course that I had wanted to do in the first place. I telephoned Paul Lowe, the director of the Traditional Chinese Medicine program at Middlesex University in London and asked if I could join. He said yes, as soon as I send the certificates of my access course results. I moved to London the following week as the course had already started and began university life.

It was terrifying and exciting to be in London! I started university and I can't express the level of anxiety that I felt. I felt like an imposter, a pretender, like I shouldn't be there. I didn't deserve to be there. I didn't belong anywhere. But I persevered because I considered it important to finish what I had started in order to apply the principle of doing something 'concrete'. In reality, it didn't really matter to me what I was doing, or where. The point was to go through the process of beginning and seeing it through to the end.

My Final Psychotic Episode – Conquering the Demons
After my first term at university, in the summer holiday, I had

the opportunity to fly to the USA to visit a friend, Michelle, who I had had a small fling with at The Barn. Michelle was beautiful and smart and I had pedestalised her hugely. I was inexperienced and insecure romantically and sexually and she was way ahead of me in that sense. I didn't have a clue about the 'dating game', how attraction works, love and romance. I tended to be obsessively romantic, naïve, needy, child-like when I developed feelings for someone and it always triggered huge feelings of insecurity for me. At other times, I could be dismissive and distant depending on the person. I discovered (a lot later!) that according to adult attachment theory, I had a 'disordered' insecure attachment type. It would have been really useful to have known about attachment theory in my 20's! I talk about attachment theory in more detail later in this guide.

In any case, this was my first ever intercontinental, solo travel flight and I was terrified of flying. I couldn't get my head around the fact that I was so far from the ground. It didn't help that there was quite intense turbulence on the way. I was on the verge of panic for half of the trip. When I arrived in Denver, I was destroyed. Even more so, when my friend showed up to meet me with her new boyfriend! It was not a good start to my trip at all. I had always wanted to travel and have exotic adventures with exotic women, but this is not what I had in mind.

I stuck it out for two weeks, staying in Boulder Colorado. Michelle was very generous and I stayed with her in the house that she was looking after in the hills around Boulder and then in an apartment in the middle of town. My desires were thwarted and I was in emotional turmoil with a jet-lag mixer. It was quite a cocktail and my fragile inner stability began to fragment once again. It was awful, and unfortunately, I couldn't appreciate at the time the fact that Boulder is a really cool place surrounded by the most beautiful mountain scenery. Later, I was to fly to New York where I stayed for a couple of nights before I went to a Dzogchen Community retreat in Massachusetts.

The retreat in Massachusetts was amazing, with Jim Valby, a teacher from the Dzogchen Community that I really valued because he helped to clarify in an experiential way, many aspects of the Dzogchen teachings that I didn't have much understanding of.

At the same time, I was discovering that my sexual energy was a strong trigger for destabilising my mental health. There were two women there who I felt a deep attraction towards and to whom I became close, but with whom I had no idea how to behave or what to do. I was so inhibited and repressed. I could not express my desires at all in a clear way and I ended up making a mess, both for myself and for them. It is funny now, looking back on it but it was really intense for me at the time. There was a huge gap between my sexual energy and desire and my ability to coordinate, communicate and channel that energy. Sexual energy is hugely powerful as we all know, and when disordered and loaded with unhealthy neurosis and fragile mental health, it can become a strong trigger. At least in my case it was like this and we will explore this topic more in the section about coordinating our energy later in this guide.

With the combination of the challenging flight to the USA, jet-lag, the awkward situation with Michelle in Boulder, the complicated sexual tension on the retreat in Massachusetts and a set of meditation practices that were quite new to me and very powerful, I once again began to become paranoid, withdrawn and to misinterpret my experiences. Towards the end of the retreat, I was beginning to lose it completely. On our way back to New York from Massachusetts, I burst out crying in the car because of the intensity of it all. I was back in my symbolic world and I was lost again.

As I was leaving New York, I waited at the bus stop for the airport which was right under the Twin Towers of the World Trade Centre. This was in June 2001. I looked up and marvelled at how vast those towers were. In my symbolic world, there was a huge battle going on in New York between various power-ful Guardians. I think it is possible that even though when in a psychotic state, we suffer from terrible delusions, there is also a heightened sensitivity that can happen, along with some moments of clarity. Maybe I picked up on something while I was in New York. On the flight on the way back, I felt like I was in danger and that the only reason that we were still in the air was because there was a spirit 'Guardian' travelling with us who was protecting us.

Back in London, I felt totally porous, like I could feel everyone in the whole city inside my body. It was a paralysing experience. My condition worsened and the city became a platform for a symbolic game in which anyone who managed to get to the end would receive a huge reward and total bliss and liberation. It was a little similar to the 'initiation' experience that I had when I was in Cornwall but on a huge London sized scale. I understand that this kind of 'porous' experience is quite a common thing for people to feel when undergoing a psychotic episode.

I realised at one point that I had to get away from all the people in the city so I took a train to Falmouth. The train journey was a continuation of 'the game' and it felt like all of the people on board were talking in some symbolic language that seemed to be related to it. I felt that I just had to keep my head down and arrive in Falmouth and ignore the things I was experiencing as much as possible.

Luckily, when I arrived in Falmouth, I was able to stay in the spare room of the house that I used to rent and it was all very familiar, but I still had the same problem as I did in London. I felt like I could feel everyone in the whole town inside my body and this symbolic game was continuing. I met with various friends and was behaving strangely around them, introverted and paranoid. It was not a good situation at all.

By this time however, I had spent seven years dealing with my condition and over this period I had developed quite extensively some of the various tools that I had received, mostly from my teacher Namkhai Norbu Rinpoche. I had at least some insight into my condition. Enough to know that I was in a bad state and that it was aggravated by being around people.

I decided to take myself away from the town to Arthur's Beach which is a walk along the coast from Falmouth. I found a grassy spot there and practiced the 8 Movements of Yantra Yoga, for around two hours. The 8 Movements are an excellent way to co-ordinate disordered energy in an individual (see the section on Coordinating and Being Present with your Energy below).

After this Yoga session, I managed to get some respite from my psychotic state and found some peace and clarity. I also started to feel rising within me a deep anger and frustration. I had been dealing with this for seven years now and it was enough. My anger became fury!

At the same time, I started to think of all of the methods for dealing with my condition that I had learned and developed over the years such as breathing techniques, meditation, using Mantras. I had managed to create enough space in myself to think of using them in a coordinated and concrete way. My fury and determination grew and I had confidence that if I applied what I had learned, that everything would be OK. I felt completely backed against a wall and I decided there and then that I would sit down and do the practices I had learned, particularly those connected with coordinating Energy using the voice (see Practical Recovery Guide section below) and I vowed not to leave my room until I had fully conquered my condition, and that is what I did.

I sat on my cushion and did the practices and I put absolutely everything into them. My whole being. All of the voices I was hearing, all of the strange sensations, everything, I relaxed into my breathing, into sound and meditation. When I began to feel tense, I got up and moved around, shook myself down and sat on my cushion again and continued. If I felt tired, I lay down, closed my eyes and relaxed. At times, huge waves of grief and tears would overcome me and I would weep. At other times, all of the experiences that came up became fuel for the fire of my meditation and instead of dominating me as they had before, only made my practice stronger and stronger.

I didn't focus overly on the specific details of the methods themselves, I had a more open, general idea, because I had discovered through my experiences in the past that if one relaxes, holding some intention, the methods will happen naturally without too much effort. This is especially true when using sound. I had had problems in the past from trying too hard with various meditation techniques which created tension and had the opposite effect to that which I wanted, making me more nervous and creating problems. This time though, I was having none of it. I let go, I used my breath, I used sound, and I relaxed and integrated my experiences.

It became clear to me that none of the voices or disordered thoughts or any of my symbolic world were anything other than my own uncoordinated, disordered energy. When I realised this, my practice became even stronger still, as it felt that I was allowing parts of myself back home to their correct places, and the more I continued, the more whole and complete I felt.

I don't know how long I stayed in the room doing these practices, maybe three or four hours but at a certain point, I knew that it was finished. I was done. It was literally as if I had flicked a switch and I was back to normal. I found it difficult to believe and tentatively made my way to visit some friends. 'You are back!' one of them said. 'How was it on the other side?'. It was clear to them that I was 'normal' again too. They could see it instantly and I was able to confidently describe what had happened to me without any paranoia or doubt. It was a revelation to me and gave me huge confidence. Especially in the teachings that I had received from Namkhai Norbu Rinpoche.

I was not hospitalised as a result of this episode and nor did I have to take medication afterwards. It was the last episode that I ever had, although there were times over the following years when I felt 'wobbly', but whenever that happened, I applied the same practices of Yoga and meditation and had no more problems.

Later that summer, I went to see Namkhai Norbu Rinpoche in Italy for a retreat of Dzoghen teachings. Interestingly, while I was there, I had a dream in which I had been sent to New York as an envoy on behalf our Community to negotiate a kind of truce with some beings who were creating problems there. In the dream, I met the representative of these beings who said that he would show me their place and how developed they were. We went down a kind of roadway into a tunnel underneath Manhattan. This roadway led to a vast underground space. Underneath New York, these beings had already created a vast city that was full of small orange lights where they lived and it was clear to me that there were no negotiations to be done here, that it was already way too late. The city was inundated. The following September 11th in a friend's apartment in London we saw the live coverage of the attacks on the Twin Towers under which I had stood at the bus stop when I was leaving New York earlier in the year.

Conclusion

My story is just an illustration of some of the kinds of things that can happen for someone who suffers from psychosis. Everyone who suffers from psychosis will have their own unique experience and also the causes of psychosis can be different. In many ways, I was fortunate in that I was always in a relatively safe environment around people who more or less had my best interests at heart. Some people are not so fortunate.

Psychosis is also an experience that is extremely common, especially among teenage pot smokers and recreational drug users. In my immediate social circle as a teenager and early twenties, at least three people that I knew had psychotic episodes and that was in a small town in Cornwall in the 1990's, before Skunk became really strong and before MDMA (Ecstasy) became mainstream. It wouldn't surprise me if that number would be much higher these days. There were also four attempted suicides, one actual suicide and two deaths from overdoses with heroin amongst my peers, one of whom was my best friend from school.

No one ever talked about mental health when I was young except to say 'xxx is mad' 'xxx went to the loony bin'. It was a taboo subject surrounded by huge ignorance. No one appeared to be educated about it and no one had anything useful to say about it. I know that things have changed a lot now and awareness of mental health issues is much more widespread but it is not a problem that is going away any time soon, especially as the world that we inhabit becomes more and more complex.

Whatever your background and whatever environment you find yourself in, I sincerely hope that the advice in this guide is easy to apply and useful for you.

PRACTICAL RECOVERY GUIDE - PART I

Crisis Mode / Being Hospitalised

The chances are that if you have discovered this guide, you may have had psychotic episodes in the past and wish to prevent a relapse, or know what to do if you do relapse. You may also be a friend or relative of someone who is unwell.

If you are feeling unwell at this time, it may be difficult for you to concentrate on reading this text. You may be hearing voices or having strange experiences. Don't worry, you can come back to it later or ask a friend to help you to understand what is written. Try your best!

Crisis Mode - Stage I: Entering the Hospital

Try your best to:

Relax, relax, relax and let go as much as you can.

Accept that you are unwell and that you need some support. It's OK. There is nothing to be ashamed of.

Try to communicate the kinds of things that you are experiencing to your doctors, nurses and carers, no matter how strange. 'I am hearing voices', 'I feel like the television is talking to me'. The more you are able to express what is going on, the less power your experiences will have over you.

Tell the doctor or nurses immediately if you feel you want to harm yourself, or others.

Trust your doctors and nurses. They are safe. They are here to care for you.

Take your medication and be patient. Your symptoms will calm down.

When you are in crisis, it is a moment that is stressful and terrifying. The strange thing is that your experiences can also seem addictive and you may not want to take medication. You need to let this go. It is not fun. It does not lead to a happy life.

We cannot function with so much stress, fear and anxiety for very long. Follow the advice of your doctor and take the medication. Wait for your symptoms to calm down. Then you can continue to use this guide to help you on your journey to good health.

Crisis Mode - Stage II:
One Day at a Time

On your first days in hospital, it is important to relax as much as possible into the routine of where you are. It will be unfamiliar to you and maybe a little scary. There is nothing that you need to do except:

Take your medication when it is given to you.

If you notice any side effects from medication like nausea or dizziness, tell your doctor or nurse immediately.

Try to eat something at meal times. This can help you to calm down.

You will still be experiencing strange things. Try not to give too much importance to them. It is difficult when they are so overwhelming, but know that they won't last.

It can be helpful to repeat positive phrases to yourself. Say them over and over again, out loud if you like, a bit like mantras. For example:

"I feel better and better every day"
"I am so much loved!"
"I will live a positive, healthy and happy life from now on"

Whatever works for you. You can make your own. You probably won't believe them at first, so just pretend. Keep saying them. Keep doing it and eventually you will start to believe them. Put your energy into it.

Rest, relax and sleep.

Sleep is important. If you cannot sleep, tell your doctor or nurse. They may be able to give you sleeping pills to help you at the beginning. There is also a section on sleep later in this guide that will help you that you can come back to.

Crisis Mode - Stage III: Getting your Feet Back on the Ground

At a certain point you will start to notice that the strange experiences that you were having are not there so much any more, but you will be feeling tired, spaced out and groggy. It will be hard to concentrate and you will have low energy and low motivation to do anything.

Now is the time that you can start to use the psychosis recovery methods in this guide to make the most of your time in the hospital. You will continue to use these methods when you go home.

Remember those movies where there has been a great storm and the crew of a huge tall ship is powerless to stop it from crashing on the rocks?

Imagine that you are the captain of one of those ships, and you survived the storm. Now you find yourself on the beach, drenched in water, exhausted and disorientated. Slowly slowly, you realise that you need to crawl up the beach, then begin to stand up. You may fall over once or twice and have to crawl again, but you survived, and you know it!

The following methods will help you to crawl up that beach and to begin to stand up and take your next steps towards life!

Being Present: The key to Everything!

Why is Being Present important? Being Present is important because it is a way of protecting your Mind, of tethering your Mind to the present moment. When you experience psychosis, there is very often a sense of disembodiment. All of these paranoias, strange thoughts, voices, delusions consume a great deal of Energy and wrap the Mind up in thoughts and feelings that are very often far removed from what you are actually practically doing right now in this present moment. Being in this state also means that our clarity gets distorted and skewed by the prism of the psychotic Mind. We need to get out of this prism.

Being Present then, brings you back to your actual reality of the here and now. What are you actually doing? You are sitting, you are walking, you are reading, you are talking, you are eating, you are sleeping, you are thinking. These are the concrete things that you are actually doing and through the practice of Being Present you constantly bring yourself back to this awareness. This process helps to protect you from flying off into your delusions especially once you become more familiar and well practiced in it.

Methods:

Being Present simply means knowing what you are doing when you are doing it. Apply this method, in a relaxed way to EVERYTHING that you do from now on. It takes some effort at first, but it gets easier and easier! Here are some examples to get you started:

Example 1 - Waking Up

When you wake up in the morning, notice it, and say to yourself 'I am awake'.

Now you will think about what you want to do next and generate the intention to do it. For example: 'I want to sit up in bed'.

Then you do the action, knowing 'I am sitting up on my bed'.

IMPORTANT: When you have completed the action, allow yourself to feel satisfied that you have done it. Try to enjoy that feeling. You have achieved something in a conscious way!

Example 2 - Brushing your Teeth

Now you think about the next thing you want to do. For example: 'I want to brush my teeth'.

Think for a while about the things that you will need to do to make this happen. This is the planning stage where you generate the intention to act.

Now you do the action, knowing what you are doing each step of the way: 'I am standing up', 'I am walking to the wash basin', 'I am picking up my toothbrush', 'I am putting toothpaste on my toothbrush', 'I am brushing my teeth', 'I am spitting out the toothpaste into the sink', 'I am rinsing my toothbrush', 'I am rinsing my mouth', 'I am putting my toothbrush down', 'I am walking back to sit on my bed'.

Now you have completed the action!

IMPORTANT: When you have completed the action, allow yourself to feel satisfied that you have done it. Try to enjoy that feeling. You have achieved something in a conscious way!

Example 3 - Getting Dressed

Another example is for getting dressed. You think to yourself 'Now I want to get dressed'.

You will think a little about what you would like to wear. Develop the intention to get dressed.

Now you enter into action and get dressed, being present every step of the way: 'Now I am putting on my socks', 'Now I am putting on my other sock', 'Now I am putting on my trousers or skirt', 'Now I am putting on my shirt' (or whatever it happens to be that you want to wear).

IMPORTANT: When you have completed the action, allow yourself to feel satisfied that you have done it. Try to enjoy that feeling. You have achieved something in a conscious way!

All of the above examples are of small achievements, but remember that all big achievements in life are simply a collection of small achievements put together, so take it one step at a time, one small victory after another. The more of these small victories you are able to make while Being Present, the more your confidence and capacity will grow.

Coordinating Your Breathing

Our breathing is a kind of bridge between our body and our mind. When we are suffering from psychosis, our Energy has become disordered and our bodies and minds have become uncoordinated, which lead us to experience strange things.

We can help ourselves to regain the coordination of our body and mind by using some simple breathing techniques (along with Being Present). The most simple way is to practice making a pause after each out-breath for a second or two. This can help us to relax, calm our minds and to reduce our feelings of fear and anxiety.

Method 1:

Sit on your bed, or in a chair. Keep your back straight and shoulders open, in a relaxed way.

Breathe in normally.

Breathe out normally.

When you get to the end of your out-breath, just pause for a second or two (don't force it!).

You can repeat this over and over again.

When you have unusual thoughts or feelings, bring your attention back to your breathing if you can. Remember to pause at the end of each breath

Method 2:
You can use counting to develop this method more.

Sit on your bed or in a chair. Keep your back straight and shoulders open, in a relaxed way.

Breathe in for a count of two.

Breathe out for a count of two.

At the end of the out-breath, remain empty for a count of two. Then repeat.

Once you have become used to this way of coordinating your breathing, you can extend the length of time that you remain empty on the out-breath to a count of three or four. Repeat over and over again.

You will become more and more familiar with this method and you will be able to use it anywhere, in almost any situation in the future to help to calm and coordinate your energy.

Crisis Mode - Stage IV: Gaining Confidence & Becoming More Active

When you are recovering from, or being in psychosis, it is very easy to become very quiet, to stay inside your head, to be overwhelmed by your experiences. As you start to feel better, you can find that you have lost your confidence and self esteem and this can feel very debilitating.

Always be kind to yourself. Respect your limits in the moment. Don't force anything, ever!

Confidence and self esteem are a bit like muscles. You can exercise them, and they will grow and become strong, although, at the beginning it can be an uncomfortable process and it will require some effort and willpower. Here are some suggestions to help you to build your confidence and self esteem:

It's Good to Talk

When you have suffered from psychosis, it can be challenging to be around other people and you may avoid talking to them. You may feel nervous or shy to say a simple hello, but interacting with people can help you 'come back' to the world.

Ask if there is a Counselling Service

Ask the doctors or nurses, when you feel ready, if it is possible to speak to a counsellor. This is one of the best ways to start to feel better and to help to get your confidence back. You can tell them everything that you are thinking and feeling, your hopes and fears. They will not judge you. They are there to listen to you and support you. If it is possible, do it, even if you are not used to sharing of yourself in this way and even if it feels strange at first!

Speak to Other Patients

You may feel nervous of speaking to other patients, but you may find that it can be helpful to socialise with them, when you feel ready. They all have their stories to tell. Even if you, or they, don't want to talk, you can do activities together like doing a puzzle or playing board games. This can also help a lot for you to gain confidence. If you or the other person begin to become agitated or uncomfortable, you can just go to your bed and lie down to rest.

Do Some Exercise Every Day

There can be a lot of sitting around in hospital, which is fine at the beginning because you need to rest and you won't feel like doing much else, but after a while, it is better to begin to do some movement every day. After all, movement is life!

Try to do Some Exercise at Least Three Times Per Day

This will depend a lot on the place where you are. If you can get outside into a garden or grounds then it is better but if you are indoors, there will probably be a small place you can find where you can do some exercises.

Try to do some exercise in the morning, after lunch and in the evening, even if it is just for two minutes each time.

Be Present! Have the intention, do the action, feel the satisfaction of having achieved your goal consciously.

If you can walk outside, it is great. Be Present! Know that you are walking.

Try some gentle stretching. Be Present! Know that you are

stretching.

Do some sit-ups or pushups. Be Present! Know that you are doing sit-ups or pushups.

Run on the spot. Be Present! Know that you are running on the spot.

Be consistent. Exercise every day. This will help you to build confidence in your body and to feel more active and engaged.

Some hospitals will have a games room where there are games like snooker or table tennis. If so, try to find someone who wants to join you. That way you get to do some exercise and be social at the same time!

Create Some Routines for Yourself

Routines can be a great way of rebuilding your foundations and your independence. You can take healthy routines with you when you leave the hospital and go home. You can use the principle of 'Being Present' mentioned above; have the intention, do the action and feel a sense of enjoyment once you have completed it and achieved your goal.

Here are some suggestions for some easy things that you can make into routines:

Make your bed in the morning when you get up or whenever you finish using it. You will see it nicely made when you come back to it. It will make you feel good.

Just before breakfast, do a small amount of exercise or stretching. Enough to get your blood flowing. This will set you up well for the day.

Eat regularly at the same times (breakfast, lunch and evening meal), even if you don't feel that hungry. When you don't feel hungry, just eat a little, or at least drink something. The Body loves rhythm.

After lunch, go for a walk (outside if you can), even if it is just five or ten minutes. You can also walk around your ward a little depending on what is possible. Try to be active, not passive.

In the mid-morning and mid-afternoon, try to find someone to share a game with you (another patient, a nurse, a visiting friend or family member). If there is a games room with a pool table or table tennis, then perfect. If not, then do a puzzle together, play cards, play a board game, play Jenga. Whatever is available that you can enjoy with someone else. You don't need to talk much if you don't want to. Just play the game.

After your evening meal, go for a walk if you can, just like you did after lunch (above).

In the evenings, try to spend some time writing down your thoughts and feelings. Your hopes, fears, worries and emotions. Don't think about it too much, just write down whatever is on your mind, even if there are some unusual thoughts and feelings. It can really help to get things out of your head and onto paper. You will feel lighter. Do it every day.

Crisis Mode - Stage V: Getting Ready to Leave the Hospital

When the time is approaching to leave hospital, it can be a little nerve-wracking. Hospital is a safe, controlled space with predictable routines where you are provided with food and shelter and you do not need to worry too much about day to day things. You will be going back into the world, with all of its various demands.

To prepare for leaving hospital, here are a few suggestions that can help to make the transition easier for you:

Try to arrange a comfortable place to stay for when you leave, before you leave. If you have a home, then you do not need to worry about this. If you do not have a home, then try to make some arrangement for a safe space with social services a friend or family member.

Start to think of some goals for your inner life as a person. What kind of person would you like to be? How would you like to feel? What might you need to do in order to achieve those things? Make a list, write it down.

Start to think of some goals and ambitions for things that you would like to do and achieve in your life. What steps might you need to take in order to make these dreams a reality? Make a list, write them down.

Now is also the time to begin to become familiar with the rest of this recovery guide (below) in order to have a map to follow that will guide you to a full recovery...

PRACTICAL RECOVERY GUIDE - PART II

After the Storm

T his section of the guide is for that moment when you have been through a crisis and received treatment for it. Your symptoms are now under control and when you try to remember what happened in your chaotic, delusional, psychotic world, it seems like you are trying to remember a dream. You remember some parts of it clearly, but most of it is out of your reach.

In a way, this is the most important section of this guide because while you are in crisis, there is really very little you can do but accept the treatment that you receive from your doctors until the symptoms have subsided. It is almost impossible to read and understand things while in a state of crisis because your interpretation of the material so easily becomes distorted by the particular psychotic vision of reality that you may be having at that time. There is no guarantee at all that you would understand any of it in the way that it is meant.

Let's take a moment to appreciate and celebrate modern anti-psychotic medicines!

One of the areas where modern medicine appears to fall down

however, is in the post crisis recovery phase. When I came out of hospital for the second time, after my month long stay, the responsibility for my treatment was passed back to my General Practitioner (GP) which means that I went to my doctor only really to get repeat prescriptions for my medication. There was no follow-up whatsoever in terms of personal interaction and I was basically on my own.

I understand that these days, people are offered courses of 6 sessions of Cognitive Behavioural Therapy (CBT) as part of their treatment (in the UK), which is fantastic and extremely useful (although 6 sessions is really the bare minimum that one needs). But at times there may be a wait of up to 6 months before they can start because there is such a long waiting list. I also understand that in some cases, certain types of family therapy and support groups are offered but it probably depends a lot on the area one lives in and how well prepared they are. All of these things are steps in the right direction, but they fall way short of a comprehensive recovery program.

BREAKING THROUGH
THE BRAIN FOG

*The More You Do, The More You
Can Do, But Don't Push It...*

The post-psychosis-crisis phase is a moment where you will feel exhausted, no doubt about it. The level of anxiety and stress that you will have been through will have been extreme. Your brain chemistry is recalibrating itself. All of this, combined with the higher doses of medication that are used to reduce your symptoms leave you feeling completely destroyed. Your symptoms may have improved and reduced significantly, but now you feel like you don't want to move. You don't want to get out of bed in the mornings, it is hard to concentrate or focus. You don't feel much about anything, you have no desire, no passion, no inspiration. I call this the 'Brain Fog'. You will have probably also lost all confidence and your self esteem will be at an all time low and you will feel like there is not much point in being active. You will also experience a strong fear of falling back into psychosis which can be paralysing. So what do you do now?

This is a tricky moment because if you remain totally passive, without a guide or plan then your recovery may be very slow and you may get stuck, like I did, for a long time in an 'in-between' state of not really being functional, but not being unwell either. At the same time, it is true that 'the more you do, the more you can do'. The problem is that if you push too much, then you can also end up taking steps backwards.

At this stage, if you have already read the section on Crisis Mode / Being in Hospital (above), this is where the principle of bringing some simple routines into our days that become habits can be really useful. Our Body, Energy and Mind all respond well to routines and this is one small way in which we can tackle coordinating them and start to become more energised. Your routine can start with simply getting up at one specific time each and every day at first and then you can develop it more as you become stronger.

Here is a re-cap of some of the routines that we mentioned earlier with a few additions.

Remember, if you are doing an activity (like making your bed or doing the washing up), set the intention first, then do the action while 'Being Present' then feel the satisfaction of completion:

Get up at the same time every single day. Choose a time and stick to it as much as possible. Set an alarm. This is important for regulating your sleep cycle which we will talk more about later.

Make your bed in the morning when you get up. You will see it nicely made when you come back to it. It will make you feel good.

Just before breakfast, do a small amount of exercise or stretching. Enough to get your blood flowing. This will set you up well for the day.

Eat regularly at the same times (breakfast, lunch and evening meal), even if you don't feel that hungry. When you don't feel hungry, just eat a little, or at least drink something. Remember, the Body loves rhythm. If your Body is happy, your Energy will be more coordinated and your Mind will be more calm.

Do the washing up after each meal and use it as an opportunity to practice 'Being Present'. Set the intention first 'I will now do the washing up'. Then do the action, all the time, knowing what you are doing. When your mind wanders into thoughts, judgements and feelings, bring it back to what you are doing and remind yourself 'I am washing up'. You can connect this with your breathing too. Then it becomes another way to coordinate your Body, Energy and Mind and something that you can turn into a habit.

With your Body, you are being present with the physical activity of washing with your hands, with your Energy, you are breathing in and out. With your Mind, you are being present and focusing on what you are doing while at the same time knowing what you are doing. If you get distracted, gently bring your mind back.

After lunch, go for a walk (outside if you can), even if it is just five or ten minutes. Be present. Appreciate the sights and smells, be thankful for the little things.

Every single day, try to have a conversation with at least one person, a friend, family member, shopkeeper. It doesn't need to be for very long. You could just say 'hello, how are you today?' and talk about the weather. The act of connecting with others in this simple way is very helpful for gradually building confidence.

After your evening meal, go for a walk if you can, just like you did after lunch.

An hour and a half before you go to sleep, switch off any computers or mobile devices that you may have and avoid anything which tends to agitate you. Do some small simple chores, some breathing exercises or read a book. This will help improve the quality of your sleep.

Later you can start to bring in some other routines as your energy starts to return and you may wish to expand them to things that you do weekly (such as go for a long walk once or twice a week, or go to the gym, or go to an art class, see a counsellor) as well as your daily routines.

Remember that regular sleep, exercise and eating are all fundamental, core routines and should as much as possible have consistent, regular times. Rhythm is important for us because it reduces stress on a basic physiological level.

CREATING THE MINDSET OF RECOVERY:

Setting Your Intention - What Does Recovery Mean to You?

After your 'Brain Fog' has lifted and you are able to think a little more clearly, it is now useful to define for yourself what recovery actually means for you. To establish a goal to aim for.

For me, recovery meant not only stabilising my condition in the medical sense to the point that I no longer experienced any symptoms and no longer needed medication, but it also meant wanting to become the best version of myself and to try to fulfill my potential as a human being as much as possible. I am still on that path! Practically speaking, that means trying my best to cultivate a healthy Body, balanced Energy, calm Mind, healthy friendships and relationships, fulfilling, satisfying work, and a sense of purpose.

Ambitious? Well, I came to the conclusion that 'health' is something that we can develop on so many different levels and that actually cultivation of 'health' is a lifetime's work! It requires thinking about the long term, being patient and not getting too attached to short term, quick fixes. I am still on my journey of recovery and in a way, writing this guide is part of it, as half the time it feels like I am writing advice to myself!

Understanding Frames of Reference: Rebuilding your House

Imagine for a moment that your Mind is like a building. When we are small babies, the foundations for the building are constructed through our early relationships with our parents, close family, teachers and guardians. As we grow and develop, the walls, roof, rooms and decorations are all created as a result of our experiences, choices and the things we absorb from our environment, our parents, family, friends and school.

After some time, the house is finished. It has a certain look and feel and personality. Later, you may be able to add an extension to the house (live with a partner, have children), do some building work (learning and education), and adapt it slightly but more or less you recognise that house as your house.

When you suffer from psychosis, it is as if a huge earthquake has shaken the house so much that it has collapsed completely and has been left as barely recognisable ruins. There may have been some small tremors beforehand that left a few cracks in the walls (nervousness, anxiety, depression) but when the full force of the quake strikes, there is not much that is recognisable left at all. All the component parts are present but they are in complete disarray, totally without context. Our frame of reference is completely broken and our minds go into a state of overdrive and panic, frantically filling the void where the solid structures used to be.

It took energy to hold that house up, to maintain it, to develop it gradually over the years, energy that we were not even consciously aware of. The forces that held the walls upright, the doors on their hinges, the windows and roof in their place. Now that the house has collapsed, all of the energy that went into holding the structure of it together needs somewhere to go. Energy cannot be destroyed, it only changes form and it is this unbridled energy that used to maintain the structure of the house that now feeds our hallucinations, fears, delusions, neuroses, fantasies, anxiety because there is no frame in which to hold it.

If you have suffered from psychosis, or are in the middle of suffering from psychosis, you may have had the experience of entering a frame of reference that is not 'yours' but finding that you can function normally, temporarily within it. Especially if it is a very strong 'frame'. For example, you may enter a doctors office and be able to very rationally and objectively describe your experiences to her and feel more or less fine while you do so, only to leave the doctors 'frame' to re-enter your psychotic state.

This is a good example of how an external frame, in this case a strong societal construct in the form of the medical system along with the doctors individual frame (which is also a strong construct) can influence us, especially if we no longer have a frame of our own. It is also an example of why we need to be careful which frames of reference we expose ourselves to, especially while we are unwell and our own frame is 'under construction', as not all frames are like those of doctors and the medical system who have our best interests at heart.

When we are recovering from psychosis, one way that we can think of it is that we are rebuilding our frame of reference, rebuilding our house. We need to rebuild from the bottom up and we will need to use some strong and reliable scaffolding to support it while we build the walls and add the roof etc.

The scaffolding we use will include medication, creating routines, having goals, self discipline, Cognitive Behavioural Therapy (CBT), counselling, Being Present, meditation, general exercise, coordinated exercise such as Yoga, Tai Chi and martial arts, eating a healthy diet, increasing healthy relationships with individuals and social groups, education, reducing contact with negative relationships, reducing and harmful bad habits, doing voluntary work, getting a job.

We need to understand that this process will take time, at least a year, like any building project, and there will be snags and problems along the way that will challenge us. We need to plan for and expect this, it should not surprise us even though it will be frustrating. We just need to continue, be patient and do our best when things become challenging.

Once we have built a strong house, it will not be moved or budged easily by outside influences because the foundations and boundaries that we keep are strong. If we let outside influences affect us, it is because it is a choice, not because our frame is so fragile that we are easily washed over by other influences that have a much stronger frame.

Some of these scaffolding components will eventually become solid walls and floors, roofs of the house and part of our daily lives.

Why use this example? Because there is an aspect of this understanding that can help protect us from future storms. From the unique insight that we have had through our experience of psychosis we can see that all frames of reference, for everyone, are very relative. They are the result of causes and conditions, they are inherently unreal because their nature is empty, we know that because we entered a state where there was no frame at all and our minds filled up the space with all sorts of distorted nonsense. We therefore do not need to get too attached to a certain way of being. We can create a strong house, but it can be flexible and open to change. We also know that apart from environmental factors that are out of our control, we as adults, can be the creators of the causes and conditions that govern our frame, we can be clear about what influences we allow into our lives with a clarity that we may not have had before. This can help us to become much more relaxed and free within ourselves once we get better.

Taking Responsibility

My teacher Namkhai Norbu Rinpoche always encouraged his students not to be passive. 'To be passive leaves one open to receiving all kinds of negativities.' This is relevant to so many different aspects of life and particularly to our recovery from psychosis. It is really important that you take responsibility for yourself and for your recovery. You have to understand that your recovery is not your doctors responsibility, it is not your family's responsibility, or your friends or your partners, it is YOUR responsibility and yours alone. If you do not take this on board right from the very start, you are already at a disadvantage going forward. You need to be brave, you need to adopt the attitude of a warrior. It is not easy to do what you are doing but you need to commit and be responsible.

This means being responsible for asking your doctors for their support and advice when you need it. When you feel like you need the support of your family and friends, it is your responsibility to ask them for help. When you know that there are services available that may be of help to you such as counselling, it is your responsibility to request them. It is important that you get into the driving seat of your recovery and start to advocate for yourself. It can be daunting at first and you also need to be aware of and respect your limits, but your efforts will be rewarded if you adopt this attitude.

This principle also applies to the smaller things in life. For example, you should take responsibility for washing our own clothes, doing your own cooking, cleaning and shopping etc. Do not be happy to let other people do these things for you all the time like parents, partner, carers etc. It is disempowering for you to let someone else do these things and will increase your passivity, eroding your capacity to act and develop skills, independence and confidence. See these small things as muscle building exercises for your new frame, strengthening the foundations of your new house. The more you do, the more you can do!

Of course, on the other hand, it is possible to take this too far and not allow anyone to do anything for you. If you do this, you may gain some independence, but it will be fragile and brittle. You need to be strong, flexible and balanced. Learning how to receive is also a valuable quality. For some people, it is not easy to accept the help of others because for whatever reason, they do not feel good enough or worthy enough to receive the help or the generosity of others. In this case, you can gently learn to allow people to support you and let them in too. It is all about balance.

Being Calm and Patient

Preponderance of the Small

Perseverance furthers.
Small things may be done; great things should not
be done.
The flying bird brings the message:
It is not well to strive upward,
It is well to remain below.

Great good fortune.

I Ching - Hsiao Kuo / Preponderance of the Small
(Richard Wilhelm Translation)

While it is important to be active, not passive, and to take responsibility for our recovery, it is also very important that we respect our limitations and remain patient. In this post-crisis moment, our condition is weakened and we cannot expect to be able to do everything we would normally do immediately. It is important that we be kind to ourselves and never ever force anything, proceeding in a relaxed but steady and consistent way. We have our long term goal of full recovery in mind but we must proceed step by step, appreciating all of the small achievements that we make along the way. If we adopt an attitude of appreciation for the small things, we can avoid falling into feeling frustrated and angry, and after all, all of the great achievements in life are created by one small step taken after another. It is important that we understand this from the very beginning of our recovery.

For every small victory that you make, take a moment to modestly appreciate it, savour it, enjoy it. Appreciation helps you to feel your happiness and joy and is also a kind of 'muscle' that you can learn to develop. Appreciation is a very good antidote for depression and anxiety which are likely to be familiar companions for you in the recovery phase of psychosis.

The Principles of Body, Energy & Mind

You may have noticed that I have often capitalised the words 'Body, Energy and Mind' above. This is a really simple and practical way of approaching how we take responsibility for our health that I have drawn from my teacher Namkhai Norbu Rinpoche. It provides a framework through which we can easily verbalise and understand processes connected with our health in general and our recovery.

In the Dzogchen teachings, there is the principle of Body, Energy (Speech) and Mind. These are known as the Three Gates and are the three aspects of our human existence. They are called 'Gates' because they are the three doorways through which we can apply methods that help us to become more healthy, balanced and free.

These three gates are interdependent. The Body affects our Energy, our Energy affects our Mind and in the same way, our Mind can affect our Energy and our Energy can affect our Body. When we suffer from an illness like psychosis, we can understand it in such a way that something has disordered the healthy interdependence of our Body, Energy and Mind, particularly our Energy system.

In Yoga traditions and also Chinese medicine related traditions such as Qigong and Tai Chi, there are systems of subtle channels in which our subtle energy flows. When everything is flowing correctly, we can perceive the world with clarity. When the flow of our Energy is disordered, our perception of the world also becomes disordered. There can be many causes of a disordered Energy system and most of them will correspond with the regular medical causes that we associate with psychosis. It doesn't really matter if we believe in Energy channels or not. It is at this point, simply a useful non-medicalised language and frame of reference to adopt that is helpful for us to visualise some parts of our recovery process.

All of the tools in this guide can be related to these three principles. In very simple terms, with regard to coordinating the Mind, we can think of using methods such as Cognitive Behavioural Therapy, Counselling, Psychotherapy, Being Present and Meditation. When we think about coordinating our Energy, we need to think mainly about the way in which we breathe and apply methods that combine breathing with movement and also 'Being Present' with our Mind. When we think about coordinating our Body, we can think in terms of doing regular exercise, creating routines, avoiding bad habits such as smoking and taking care with our diet.

Reducing Negative Influences

We are all familiar with the expression 'you are what you eat', but when you think about it, it does not only apply to food but anything you choose to consume with the attention of your Body, Energy and Mind. For example, when you spend a lot of time with a particular group of people, after some time, you will tend to reflect, adopt and share their mental attitudes and their habits if for no other reason than just to 'fit in'. You will want to harmonise with your environment and for this reason it is important to think about what kinds of environments you want to place yourself in.

Now you need to ask yourself if the world view and habits that you have adopted are in fact healthy for you. Have you adopted them as a result of your own reflections and conclusions, or only because they are the causes and conditions that surround you in your immediate environment and you have never questioned them? You need to understand that you can choose what kind of environment you wish to place yourself in and that it is very important for your mental health to surround yourself with healthy, positive influences. This includes the kinds of things you expose yourself to on social media, the internet, TV and films.

Ask yourself which people, activities, foods, habits (including self-talk) etc in your life agitate your condition and those which help you to feel more healthy, balanced and calm. You now need to take steps to reduce or remove all influences that are not helpful for you.

This process can require you to be extremely brave because very often, there are people, places and things that are not good for you at all that you continue to be around because they are comfortable through their familiarity. They are what you know, and changing them can be very scary, while at the same time, there can be a huge fear of slipping back into psychosis, so you want to be around familiar things. You may feel that it is a case of 'better the devil you know'.

You may need to gradually remove yourself from your usual circle of friends if they have very negative attitudes, drink heavily, take drugs or engage in violence, and forge new relationships with people who are more constructive. You may need to, at least temporarily, distance yourself from your family or partner if they are abusive or have attitudes and beliefs that are limiting for your recovery.

Reducing negative influences alone is not enough. We should replace them with something else, otherwise this will be a much more difficult process. The other thing to remember is that it is not possible to do everything at once. It is really important to respect your limitations and proceed gradually.

Action:

The most simple thing you can do here is to constantly ask yourself the question: Is this situation or influence good for me?

If the answer is 'No, it is not good for me' then ask yourself how you can gradually remove yourself from this situation and not have to enter it again in the future.

If the answer is 'Yes, it is good for me', then ask yourself if there are ways that you can increase your exposure to that situation or similar ones in the future.

You absolutely HAVE to put yourself first at this point in your recovery. Your health should be your top priority at this time. If you do not look after your health now, there is no way that you can be useful to anyone else in the future. Of course there may be some circumstances where someone is dependent on you such as your children etc where you need to put them first, and being responsible for others can be helpful for your recovery also if approached with a healthy attitude, but in general, you should focus on what is good for you. Your Body, Energy and Mind.

Action:

Make a list of all the major negative influences in your life that you are aware of. You can categorise them into areas such as people, habits, places etc. It can help to list them because a) making lists in this way helps to increase your clarity and b) there may be some aspects of your life that are not good for you that you have not acknowledged for yourself and the act of writing these things down can bring them out.

You can also make some red and yellow flags for each of them. Red flags being things that you need to actively avoid and Yellow Flags being things that you can work on distancing yourself from or changing your relationship with over time. Be specific. For example:

People: who are always putting you down – Yellow Flag, who are always judging and criticising – Yellow Flag, who are passive aggressive – Yellow Flag, who are abusive, violent or dangerous – Red Flag, who are always high – Red Flag.

Habits: unhealthy / comfort eating – Yellow Flag, smoking cannabis – Red Flag, smoking cigarettes – Yellow Flag, taking cocaine and other recreational drugs – Red Flag, not exercising – Yellow Flag.

Places: that make you feel nervous or agitated – Yellow Flag, places that are physically dangerous for you – Red Flag.

Increasing Positive Influences

N ow, using the principle of 'you are what you eat', you have thought about what negative influences you can begin to remove or reduce. Using the same logic, you can think 'ok, if I increase positive, productive, healthy influences in my life, I will become more positive, productive and healthy!'

You can think about all of the things in your life that you consider to be positive influences. Your positive influences could be very simple like enjoying the way the sun rises or sets, enjoying walking in nature, enjoying breathing, enjoying dancing, enjoying the company of certain friends who make you feel good and nourished when you are around them. Make a list, and take a special moment to develop a strong sense of appreciation for those things. Appreciation is an underrated emotion that helps us to combat anxiety and depression, and like all emotions, it is like a muscle, so cultivate your appreciation muscles.

Positive influences can also take the form of introducing plants or pets into your home. Plants are life and growth and nourishment, giving off oxygen, absorbing carbon dioxide, cleansing and purifying our environment, all good things that can have a good effect on your wellbeing long term. Pets provide company and we also need to be responsible for them and take care of them, which can provide a great sense of routine and structure to our lives.

Now look at your list of existing positive influences and think a little about how you might be able to increase them. For example, if you like plants, maybe you could start gardening for fun. If you don't have a garden, maybe you know someone you could ask who does. You could watch Youtube videos on gardening to educate yourself in the best ways to do it, or go to the library and study some gardening books. If you have certain friends who you feel good around, maybe you can try to spend more time with them.

Maybe you feel like there is nothing positive whatsoever in your life and that you can't think of anything to put on a list. In this case, don't worry. Now is the time to gently create them by introducing some of the methods in this guide. Remember, you are responsible for your recovery. It is empowering to take control and to own your recovery process. You can do it. It will take some time, patience, and yes, discipline, but you can do it!

Restricting Unnecessary Information Intake

When you are recovering from psychosis, you need to cultivate positive states of Body, Energy and Mind. You also need to construct a strong, healthy frame of reference in order to engage effectively with the circumstances around you.

The last thing that you need while you are 'painting your house' is to set up a water cannon next to it and spray it with water while the paint is still wet. It may be fine once the paint has dried, but while you are painting, it would be completely counterproductive and just damage your good work. Not to mention that you still have your scaffolding in place and the power of the water cannon could knock it all down.

It's a silly analogy I know, but checking your Facebook / Instagram / Twitter / whatever news feed all the time is a bit like spraying a water cannon at your 'under construction' frame of reference. Most media, including the news at this stage in your recovery is just noise and is not helpful for you. It fills your head with useless static that consumes your Energy and fills your Mind with tension. All of these outlets are hotbeds of confusion, distortion and manipulation. They are after all businesses and exist in order to make money from your attention. Of course there are moments of clarity there too, but while you are in a vulnerable state, it is harder to distinguish what is distortion and what is clarity. Very little that is constructive can come out of putting your precious Energy in there at this point.

How many times have you casually been scrolling through your

Facebook News Feed and then found that you have just lost half an hour of your life and you haven't gained anything except a bad physical posture, a sense of agitation and a nagging feeling that everyone else's life is so much better than yours?

Have you ever tried not watching the news or reading a newspaper for an extended period of time? Did it make such a huge difference to your life that you missed out? I don't think so. Unless your work (if you are well enough to work) involves needing to stay up to date with current affairs, my guess is that restricting your information intake made no difference at all to your life and positively reduced a good amount of the mental 'noise' you experienced. The same goes for Social Media. All of these outlets thrive on creating drama and tension, and that is exactly what you do not need.

Social Media is also a rabbit hole in the sense that it can become easy to live your life vicariously through your imagination, by projecting yourself onto other people's memes, photos, tweets, videos and blogs rather than having real experiences for yourself. When you are recovering from psychosis, it can be very tempting to get drawn into this because you will feel introverted and will lack confidence and motivation, so it will feel easier to live through other people in the Social Media world.

What you need at this point are concrete relationships, interactions and friendships with actual physical people to help you to establish and rebuild your frame of reference. You do not need digitally mediated experiences that are curated by people's vanity and need to sell you stuff or gain revenue through advertising clicks.

Did I mention Netflix? I love Netflix and other video streaming sites, they are like a warm blanket of escape, especially TV series these days. 'I'll just watch one more...' sound familiar..? But just think how much time you lose watching films online and TV series. One film is an hour and a half of our life. One TV series season is more or less 12 hours! How many of these do you watch each year? Try adding up the amount of hours. Is this the best use of your time?

I am not saying that I don't think you should ever watch films and TV, but I do recommend limiting the amount of time you allow yourself to do this. I also recommend trying to find a friend or two to watch shows together with, so that it becomes a shared, social activity. If you are a gamer, try to play multi-player games where you can have someone else in the room with you playing as well (not just other gamers online).

The other danger with these activities apart from losing time and filling your head with noise is that they can increase your isolation. You are probably being alone while you watch or play and therefore you are not developing your confidence or growing your self esteem and social skills which is not helping you. Be aware of this.

Action:

If you find yourself glued to your television, laptop, tablet or smartphone, game console every spare second you get, stop it! If you must dive into the digital rabbit hole then limit your exposure time to 30 minutes per day of social media and 1 hr of relaxing TV/streaming/gaming.

Honestly, it is best to get your head out of the screen and do some more constructive things with real people, go for a walk, do some sport, stretching or Yoga. If you must spend time online, make good use of it by educating yourself, start to learn a language, watch some tutorials, learn some re-cipes, gain some knowledge and skills, make it work for you and nourish you.

Time is precious and your energy is limited so use it wisely. You can use TV time or Social Media time as a reward for hav-ing done something more constructive.

BEING PRESENT:
YOUR NEW JOB

I have mentioned 'Being Present' in the Crisis Mode section above. It really is the cornerstone of the recovery process, so we are going to go deeper into it here.

If you forget everything else in this book, remember 'Being Present'. From now on, you need to treat Being Present as your role in life, your job, your purpose until you reach a point where you no longer even need to try. It is just something that you do. It is part of you. So what is it?

As I mentioned before, Being Present is very simple. It means that you know what you are doing when you are doing it. Easy right?

Being Present with Physical Stuff (Body)

Ok, well maybe this is a little easier than some of the other types of presence. The trick is, as with all forms of Being Present is number one, to actually remember to do it!

For example, right now, I know that I am sitting on my sofa, writing this text on my laptop which in this moment is actually on my lap and is starting to feel a bit too warm for comfort. I am also aware that it is not great for my posture to stay in this position. But I can sum this up by simply knowing 'I am sitting and writing'.

What are you doing right now?

Your answer will probably be that you are being somewhere (sitting down, standing), reading this guide. If your answer is more complicated, it is time to simplify. What are you literally doing right now?

So let's exercise this Being Present muscle a little more. Why? Because when we suffer from psychosis, we can have very strong experiences with our Body, Energy and Mind and if we do not have any capacity to relax and allow these experiences to arise and pass away, we get totally drawn into them, into the story of them, or if there is no story, our Mind will create one no matter how bizarre. When we develop our capacity to Be Present with these experiences, we can allow them to come and go without getting so involved and falling 'through the looking glass'. As this capacity grows, it can become much easier to maintain a calm state and be able to create some space around our experiences which allows us to have more choice over whether they affect us or not.

In the Crisis Mode guide above, I took you step by step through some simple physical tasks that happen every day. Here they are again to remind you followed by some more. Remember, these are just a few examples of being present with your Body to give you some inspiration but you need to apply this principle as much as possible, in a relaxed way, to all of your experiences:

Example 1 - Waking Up
When you wake up in the morning, notice it, and say to your-

self 'I am awake'

Now you will think about what you want to do next and generate the intention to do it. For example: 'I want to sit up in bed'.

Then you do the action, knowing 'I am sitting up on my bed'.

IMPORTANT: When you have completed the action, allow yourself to feel satisfied that you have done it. Try to enjoy that feeling. You have achieved something!

◆ ◆ ◆

Example 2 - Brushing your Teeth

Now you think about the next thing you want to do. For example: 'I want to brush my teeth'.

Think for a while about the things that you will need to do to make this happen. This is the planning stage where you generate the intention to act.

Now you do the action, knowing what you are doing each step of the way: 'I am standing up', 'I am walking to the wash basin', 'I am picking up my toothbrush', 'I am putting toothpaste on my toothbrush', 'I am brushing my teeth', 'I am spitting out the toothpaste into the sink', 'I am rinsing my toothbrush', 'I am rinsing my mouth', 'I am putting my toothbrush down', 'I am walking back to sit on my bed'.

Now you have completed the action!

IMPORTANT: When you have completed the action, allow yourself to feel satisfied that you have done it. Try to enjoy that feeling. You have achieved something!

◆ ◆ ◆

Example 3 - Getting Dressed

Another example is for getting dressed. You think to yourself 'Now I want to get dressed'.

You will think a little about what you would like to wear. Develop the intention to get dressed.

Now you enter into action and get dressed, being present every step of the way: 'Now I am putting one of my socks', 'Now I am putting on my other sock', 'Now I am putting on my trousers or skirt', 'Now I am putting on my shirt' (or whatever it happens to be that you want to wear).

IMPORTANT: When you have completed the action, allow yourself to feel satisfied that you have done it. Try to enjoy that feeling. You have achieved something!

Remember, these are just simple examples, but we can apply presence to absolutely everything we do. In any given day, there are countless opportunities for us to Be Present with our Body. Here are some more...

◆ ◆ ◆

Example 4 - Breakfast:

I am walking into the kitchen

I am speaking to my friend

I am making breakfast

I am sitting down

I am eating breakfast

I am getting up

I am washing up my breakfast things

◆ ◆ ◆

Example 5 - Going to the Shop

I am walking down the street

I am entering the shop

I am looking for (enter shopping list item here...)

I am placing (shopping list item) into my basket

I am looking for (enter shopping list item here...)

I am placing (shopping list item) into my basket

etc.

I am queueing at the checkout

I am paying at the checkout

I am leaving the shop

I am walking down the street with my shopping

I am entering my house

I am putting my shopping away

◆ ◆ ◆

Example 6 - Going to Sleep

I am getting changed into my sleeping clothes

I am walking to the bathroom

I am washing

I am walking to my bedroom
I am getting into my bed
I am lying down
I am going to sleep

◆ ◆ ◆

Coordinating & Being Present with your Energy

Coordinating and Being Present with your Energy is a little more subtle and subjective than Being Present with your Body. When you are Being Present with physical things, it is obvious what you are doing. When you stand up, there is no question that you are standing up. When you are eating, you are obviously eating. The Energy level is not quite like that because it may not always be easy to name your experiences, because the experience of Energy is somewhere in between the Body and the Mind and can include sensations, feelings and also emotions.

In Eastern traditions like Chinese medicine, Tibetan medicine and Yoga, there is a very rich language for describing things on the Energy level, but in the West, we do not have such a strong frame of reference for these things but very basically for the purposes of this guide, coordinating and Being Present with our Energy means coordinating and Being Present with our breathing. Have you ever noticed that when you feel very nervous or agitated that your breathing is very shallow and rapid? And when you are calm and relaxed, your breathing is slow and deep?

The first thing that we need to do in order to coordinate our breathing is to simply place our awareness there. Below are some simple examples of how connected our Energy level is with our breathing and how to Be Present with it.

Simple Breathing Method

Whenever you are not thinking about anything in particular

or not doing anything in particular, (remember, Being Present is now your job, so there is always something to do!) bring your attention in a very relaxed way to your breathing. It is good at this point also to straighten your back, in a relaxed way, because this helps to keep you alert. Don't try to control or judge your breathing. Simply be aware of it. Feel the sensation in your nostrils as you breathe in and out and the feeling of the air entering and leaving your Body as you breathe in and out. The whole process of breathing in and breathing out. You may notice other sensations in your Body that can be comfortable, uncomfortable or neutral or certain tendencies in your Mind like agitation, anger, desire, fogginess or clarity that affect the way you feel in your Energy. In any case the main point here is to gently be Be Present with and aware of your breathing so always bring yourself back to that, whatever else is going on.

If you find that you have become caught up in some kind of thought cascade, a mental story, the first thing to do is notice. Then, gently bring yourself back to your awareness of your breathing. Do this again and again in a relaxed way. Make it a habit. Make it your job!

When I used to live in London, I liked to do this kind of thing on the Tube / Metro, or on buses. You can find those moments that punctuate your day like travel, going to the bathroom, walking etc and put them to good use by Being Present with your breathing.

Coordinated Breathing Methods

I mentioned the first two of these methods in the crisis mode section above. Here they are again as a reminder. Very simply speaking, the principle to remember is that if you remain empty for longer on the out-breath, your Energy becomes more relaxed and as a result your Mind also becomes more relaxed and calm:

❖ ❖ ❖

Method 1:

Keep your back straight and shoulders open, in a relaxed way.

Breathe in normally.

Breathe out normally.

When you get to the end of your out-breath, just pause for a second or two (don't force it!).

You can repeat this over and over again.

When you have any types of thoughts or feelings, unusual or otherwise, bring your attention back to your breathing if you can. Remember to pause at the end of each

❖ ❖ ❖

Method 2:

You can use counting to develop this method more.

Sit on your bed or in a chair. Keep your back straight and shoulders open, in a relaxed way.

Breathe in for a count of two.

Breathe out for a count of two.

At the end of the out-breath, remain empty for a count of two. Then repeat.

◆ ◆ ◆

Once you have become used to this way of coordinating your breathing, you can extend the length of time that you remain empty on the out-breath to a count of three or four. Repeat over and over again.

You will become more and more familiar with this method and you will be able to use it anywhere, in almost any situation in the future to help to calm and coordinate your energy.

Being Present with and Coordinating your Energy through the Voice: Affirmations, Mantras and Prayers

Our voice is an extension of our breathing. We cannot speak if we do not use our breath. We can therefore understand that because breathing relates to our Energy level, then the things that we say can have a positive or negative effect on our Energy. If we sing a song that we like, we may feel good sensations in our Body, and our Mind may become more relaxed. If we engage in criticising, mocking and vilifying people, afterwards, we may feel uncomfortable with our Energy, agitated, tainted or nervous.

If we extend this idea that the way in which we use our voice can affect our Energy and consequently our Mind, we can begin to understand how affirmations and also, Mantras and prayers work. All of these can be used as sounds that are repeated over and over again with the voice that are imbued with positive qualities that with repeated practice can have a profound and positive effect on our Energy and Mind in particular. I personally use Mantras a lot because I have a connection with the Tibetan Buddhist tradition, but whether you follow a spiritual path or not, you can find or create a series of words that embody qualities that you wish to develop in yourself. With extensive repetition, using your voice you will be able to have a positive coordinating effect on your Energy.

Using Your Voice Effectively

Firstly, you need to choose an affirmation, Mantra or prayer that is easily repeatable over and over again. It is also important to be careful to choose words with meanings that you wish to embody, that are relevant to your health and recovery and that will not cause problems for you!

To use your voice effectively to coordinate your Energy, it is not enough simply to repeat the sounds alone and to be completely distracted in every other way. For this principle to really work well, you need to enter deeply into the sound with your whole being. That sound becomes like a kind of washing machine into which you feed the totality of your Body, Energy and Mind.

With your Body, you let the physical sensations that you are feeling fully combine with the sound that you are pronouncing with your breath. You need to ride those sensations with your breathing. Breathe the words of your affirmation, Mantra or prayer into all of your physical sensations and energetic feelings. Move around if you need to, get up, shake your body, sit down again, lie down, all the time riding the sound, letting it wash through you totally, relaxing and relaxing all the way.

Whenever you feel tension in your Body or Energy, you need to relax. Use the sound to enter into your sensations of tension. Leave no stone unturned. Embrace everything that arises no matter how unpleasant or uncomfortable. Don't judge if what you are feeling is good or bad, simply use your breath, use the vibration of the sound to enter into your sensations and relax. Sometimes, you will need to take a rest. Just drop it at this point and relax. Lie down. Wander around. Drink some tea. Then come back to it. Remember, you are coordinating your Energy and coordinated energy is relaxed Energy so it is important not to charge up and get all tense.

With your Mind, whatever thoughts and feelings you have, no matter how boring, exciting, normal, crazy, agitated, simple or complicated they are, you need to gently direct it, using your breath, into the words that you are using and deeply through any physical sensations that you may have. Very often, certain thought clusters and cascades will have a direct correspondence with certain parts of your body. When you notice this, you need to literally breathe the sound of the affirmation, Mantra or prayer into the thought and its associated physical and energetic sensations, all the time relaxing, relaxing and relaxing.

Affirmations in particular can be a good way to reverse negative self talk patterns by replacing that internal dialogue habit with something else that is more constructive. You can create any kind of affirmation you like making sure that they embody positive, healthy qualities that you wish to develop in your life.

Here are some affirmations like those that I used when I was in hospital at one point. They are very simple and helped me at that time. Of course you can create any affirmation that you like, or do a search online for affirmations where you will be sure to find one that fits your needs:

I am living a wise, happy and positive life

I am getting better and better every day

I am loving and I am loved

Coordinating your Energy and Being Present with Exercise

Worms will not eat living wood where the vital sap is flowing;
Rust will not hinder the opening of a gate when the hinges are used each day.
Movement gives health and life.
Stagnation brings disease and death.

Proverb in Traditional Chinese Medicine
(Source: Wisdom in the Body by Michael Kern)

With all of the following methods, you will find that some learning is required which ideally will involve you initially going to a class. Going to classes is good because they help you to build your social skills and confidence while being united with other people around a common purpose, which is to learn something. I highly recommend it.

Your aim with these methods should be to learn enough so that you can do them by yourself at home whenever you want to and not to be dependent on the class. These are life skills and companions that you will learn and take forward with you into your old age. I recommend choosing one that you connect with strongly at first and developing it deeply. Whatever you choose should become a personal practice for you. Of course you don't need to learn all of them, as you will feel like you connect with some things more than others, so it is good to find a method that you connect with and develop it enough so that you can make it your own. There may also only be limited options to choose from in your local area.

The Eight Movements of Yantra Yoga

Previously, I mentioned doing some Yoga movements that helped me to calm my Mind and Energy and to overcome the last episode of psychosis that I had. The method I used is called the Eight Movements of Yantra Yoga. These Eight Movements are used specifically to purify the Prana or Energy system of the body helping it all to flow in the correct way. They are a great way of coordinating the Body, Energy and Mind because they combine rhythmic physical movements with specific breathing methods and holding of the breath which gives the Mind a focus of attention resulting in the generation of a profoundly calm state.

Once you have learned The Eight Movements, they are very easy to use on a daily basis wherever you are. You can repeat them over and over again and feel the positive effects accumulating. They are probably the single best method that I have found for coordinating my Energy.

Learning Yantra Yoga:

There are various Yantra Yoga teachers around the world. The main Yantra Yoga website is a good place to start to try and find someone in your area: www.yantrayoga.net

There are also books and videos on Yantra Yoga that you can purchase (see Resources section below)

Yoga Sun Salutes

One of the classic Yoga routines that is taught in most Yoga classes is the Sun Salute. The Sun Salute is a great method to learn because it is simple and easy to apply and has the function of coordinating your Energy. Once you have learned the Sun Salute you can do it every day, and even if it is the only Yoga that you ever learn, you can repeat it and repeat it again and again, for hours and hours if you have the possibility, and it will become more and more profound for you, helping to calm your Mind and increase your clarity. It is also a great preparation for other more demanding Yoga postures. The Sun Salute is probably the easiest coordination method to find classes for, and that you can learn and use at home easily. You can probably also learn it by watching Youtube videos although I do not recommend this.

Different Yoga Systems

I recommend learning Yantra Yoga because I have much more experience with it than other systems of Yoga, but everyone is different and what suits one person may not suit another. That is after all why there are so many different systems that we can choose from. When choosing a Yoga system, I would recommend going for traditional styles like Hatha Yoga or Iyengar Yoga as they are more connected with the original roots of Yoga practice. Other systems like Ashtanga are also good if you like to be a bit more dynamic and athletic.

To get the most benefit out of any type of Yoga postures, it is necessary to combine your movement with breathing. This is already excellent for coordinating your Energy.

In many traditional systems of Yoga, there are exercises called Pranayamas that help to go much deeper into breathing. These are excellent ways of learning how to work with breathing and to understand breathing principles and how they relate to your Energy. Be careful though never to force anything to do with breathing practices. There is a real danger of damaging your Energy and making yourself more nervous and agitated if you do, so be careful and try to find an experienced teacher!

Tai Chi & Qigong

Tai Chi and Qigong are deep and profound systems with a long history which are connected with the Chinese Medical system and its Taoist roots. If you connect with a good teacher and have an affinity for these practices then they can be your companions throughout your life. Qigong in particular has a direct connection with coordinating the breathing and Energy system. It is fairly easy to find Tai Chi and Qigong classes in local community centres in many countries. You will use slow, gentle movements coordinated with breathing and sometimes visualisations, all of which help you to enter a profoundly calm and coordinated state.

Again, if you decide to learn Tai Chi, Qigong or both, I recommend learning by heart a routine or collection of routines that you can easily use at home and do them on a daily basis. This kind of activity helps you to build the 'foundations' of your new frame of reference and provide you an activity which is by you and for you and which is not dependent on your circumstances. Whatever happens in your outer circumstances, more or less you can continue to apply these practices and make them part of your routine.

Harmonious Breathing System

There is a system of breathing that has been developed by one of my Yantra Yoga teachers, Fabio Andrico called Harmonious Breathing. This is an excellent way of learning how to breathe in a more coordinated and profound way and it is very easy to apply. There is a book, video and various online resources that you can explore. Fabio is one of the main teachers of Yantra Yoga worldwide and has a huge breadth and depth of experience so I can happily recommend the Harmonious Breathing system.

Martial Arts

Martial arts are not quite so directly focused on coordinating Energy but they do have that effect indirectly because in order to perform a martial art, you are required to move your Body in a coordinated way with a strong focus of Mind, which combined, helps to coordinate your Energy. There are many different types of martial arts: Kendo, Kyudo (archery), Judo, Karate, Kung Fu, Jiu Jitsu and Aikido are some of them.

Learning a martial art will also greatly boost your confidence as it is a social activity, something that you need to do in a group, that as you develop will help you to feel a sense of confidence with your Body and Mind that comes along with training and discipline. They are also a good way to channel negative emotions like aggression and anger.

Being Present with your Mind

Now we get to the juicy stuff! Being Present with the Mind can be really challenging. Our Minds are always busy, especially when we have been suffering from psychosis where our minds have become wrapped up inside themselves similar to the way a piece of paper can be folded in order to make shapes in Origami. It is just paper, but it looks like something that is not paper, and it was probably looking pretty monstrous for a while when you were very unwell.

Hopefully at this stage, your symptoms have calmed down and you can apply these methods. Otherwise, come back to this when you are ready. Remember, never force anything. You can push a little, but don't force anything.

Method I – Like a Bear Catching Salmon

The most simple method here is a little like when bears catch salmon in a river. Bears will stand in the river and wait for the salmon to pass and quickly catch them as they dart and jump through the water. In this case, you are the bear and your thoughts are the salmon.

All you have to do is every time that you notice a thought coming along, catch it by saying to yourself 'I am thinking', then relax. It doesn't matter what the thought is about or what the story is behind it. None of that matters. All you need to do is catch it with 'I am thinking'. Then you just relax. You don't need to judge the thought, you don't need to follow the thought and get into the story of it. Then when the next one comes along, you do it again, and again, and again, and again (remember, Being Present is now your job!). Don't forget to relax after you have recognised that you are thinking. Relaxing is the most important part.

Examples:

(thought process) I'm really hungry and I really want to eat some nice tuna fish but I don't have any at home. I should... BOOM – catch yourself and say to yourself 'I am thinking' then just try to relax.

(thought process) I am sure all these people were talking about me before I entered the room saying this and that... BOOM – catch yourself, say to yourself 'I am thinking' and try to relax. Remember, it is now your job to be present. It does not matter at all what the content of your thoughts are. Only that you catch them and understand 'I am thinking'.

(thought process) This sunset is really beautiful, I'd like to... BOOM – Catch yourself. 'I am thinking' then relax without judgement.

(thought process) So and so is so attractive but I don't think it could work between us, they... BOOM – catch yourself. Don't judge. Just say to yourself 'I am thinking'. Observe the fact that you are thinking and simply relax.

Get the idea? You can even see it as a kind of game that you can play every time you remember. Maybe sitting on a bus or walking down the street, or sitting in your room. You could also schedule some time to practice this every day, adding it to your routine, even If it is just for five or ten minutes and develop it so that it becomes a habit.

Being Present with Negative Emotions

I have included Being Present with negative emotions here

alongside the Mind section, but of course we cannot separate them from the Energy level because very often emotions arrive with some kind of Energy sensation that we feel. Very often, strong emotions will have a physical, Body level manifestation too, classic examples being having digestive problems when we get upset, or needing to pee frequently when we are nervous or anxious.

If we observe well, we can see that the root of negative emotions will start with an initial thought that appears as a reaction to a particular cause. That initial thought will spark another thought and then another. The thoughts cascade into a kind of thought story which grows and feeds itself bouncing off previous thought patterns that are related based on your prior experiences. As this cascade of thoughts grows and spreads out from the Mind level and connects with the Energy level, it develops into negative emotions like anger (I don't like something), attachment / craving (I like something and I want it), pride (I am better than someone or something) and jealousy (someone or something else is better than me).

Why should you Be Present with these emotions? Negative emotions when they become strong enough can, feed themselves and lead to negative actions. If left unchecked, the thought process will move from the Mind level into the Energy level and then into the Body level where actions are carried out. Generally actions that are rooted in negative emotions are not going to be positive and will lead to negative consequences, either for ourselves or others, so it is better that negative emotions do not grow to the point where they dominate us too much.

When we suffer from psychosis, our negative emotions can become really extreme and at their worst can lead to thoughts of harming others or ourselves. When we hear voices that are persecutory for example and have other similar experiences, it is partly because we have accumulated huge levels of negative emotions like anger and resentment over many years that we have not been able to allow ourselves to feel, process, acknowledge or express. We did not have the tools at the time to deal with them, and now they are bursting out of us like an explosion. But, because they are our own 'homeless', unprocessed energy, they cannot go anywhere, so we begin to experience them as something external in the form of voices, delusions and other strange distorted experiences. Part of the process of recovering from psychosis in my experience is learning how to effectively reintegrate the energy of these emotions and to work with emotions effectively.

When we suffer from psychosis, we can feel very strong anger, sadness, anxiety, desire and all emotions. If we can develop a strong Being Present 'muscle' with our emotional states, it can help to prevent us from falling into being totally swamped by them. It doesn't mean that we should block our emotions. I am not saying that. It is very important that we feel them, embrace them fully and allow them space to come up. Otherwise, we will externalise them and turn them in on ourselves, or project them onto the people around us. We need to accept that they are part of us. If we repress them or block them, they will find ways to come out anyway. It is better to meet them head on if we can. We need to feel them and integrate them into our experience.

Method: Noticing, Naming and Relaxing

What is important here is the recognition, allowing yourself to feel the sensation of the specific emotion, naming it, trying not to enter into judgement about it, or the story around it. This process takes some of the power away and allows you some space to relax.

The other important thing to remember not just here, but always, is that nothing whatsoever is permanent! So we may as well relax, because sooner or later, what we are feeling will pass. We may feel a very strong emotion in one moment, and when we are in that state, we feel that we need to do something, to act in order to make it go away because we don't want to feel it, especially if it is a truly terrible feeling, but we should try to remember that nothing lasts forever and that the best thing that we can do is to try to relax and to continue to gradually coordinate our Body, Energy and Mind.

Examples:

Someone gives you some unsolicited advice that annoys you on multiple levels. BOOM catch yourself. Notice that you are angry and resentful. Say to yourself 'I am angry'. Feel the sensation fully, don't block it. Try to relax. Do not judge if it is good or bad. Just notice it, be aware of it, feel it, accept it, embrace it and relax.

You are walking down the street and see a beautiful flower growing in someone's garden and you feel a strong urge to pick the flower and bring it back to your house to put in a vase. BOOM catch yourself. Notice that you feel desire and attachment. Say to yourself 'ah.. I am feeling desire and attachment towards this flower'. Feel the sensation of the desire, don't block it, allow it space to be and simply relax. You do not need to act. Just notice, embrace it and relax.

While waiting for a bus, someone pulls up right next to the bus stop in a beautiful Tesla car. You would love to have that car, but right now, there is no way that it is possible for you to buy. Also the person driving the car looks so healthy and happy and is with a partner who looks amazing too. You think that their lives are much better than yours and that you are such a failure in comparison. BOOM catch yourself. Notice that you are jealous. Say to yourself 'I am jealous'. Feel the sensation fully in your body, don't block it. Try to relax and simply Be Present without judging if it is good or bad.

You are talking to someone and they say something that you think is just ridiculous. In your Mind, you are thinking 'this person is such a moron'. On a much deeper level, you are thinking 'because this person is such a moron, I am so much better than them!' BOOM catch yourself. Notice that you are feeling pride. Feel the sensation in your body. Notice how it makes you feel and say to yourself 'I am feeling pride'. Don't judge whether it is good or bad, simply relax and be present with the emotion. Don't block it. Allow it, embrace it and relax.

Sometimes you will feel emotional but you are not able to name what it is that you feel. In this case don't worry! You can name that as the emotion of feeling confused. You can notice 'I am confused' and try to relax. It is ok to be confused. It is normal for everyone.

Putting it all Together

Ok, now that you have gained some experience with Being Present with Body, Energy and Mind, now it is time to put it all together. This 'job' of Being Present should be applied dynamically as much as possible to all situations in your life. This means that as you go through your life, you cycle through these methods of Being Present according to your circumstances throughout the day. Of course you will be distracted and caught up in experiences, this is normal and there is no need to fight that. What we are talking about here is developing a habit that will eventually permeate everything you do. In order to develop the habit, we can learn to remember to use the gaps in our distraction to apply the methods.

Examples:

Here are a few really simple examples of how we can cycle through experiences and apply methods throughout a day. It is basically a process of constantly bringing yourself back to your 'job' of Being Present:

Waking Up – I know that I am awake

Getting Up – I become aware of my breathing and put my attention on that as I get dressed and wash etc.

Eating Breakfast – I become totally distracted because I am talking to my friend (it is really hard in my experience to remain present while having conversations. Maybe it will be easier for you!). Eventually I notice 'I am talking with my friend'.

Nervousness and Anxiety – The conversation I had with my friend left me feeling nervous and anxious for no real reason that I could identify. My Energy feels disordered so I recognise 'I feel nervous and anxious' and try to relax. As I am walking around getting on with my day after breakfast, I put my attention on my breathing for a while, gently being aware of the sensation of breathing in and breathing out in order to help coordinate my Energy.

Walking – With my Body, I know that I am walking. With my Energy, I am aware of my in and out breaths. With my Mind, I am aware that I am starting to think about the things that I need to do in my day. I catch myself. 'I am thinking' and relax, continuing to walk. (I am a big fan of going for walks because they are an opportunity to practice Being Present with all three aspects, Body, Energy and Mind without too many obstacles.)

Checking Facebook – I open Facebook. I get totally drawn in to the useless stuff I see in my newsfeed hoping that if I keep scrolling, I might find some things that are interesting. I find some semi-interesting stuff and click on some links but none of it is really very good quality information. I am totally distracted. I realise that I am totally distracted and say to myself, 'I am totally distracted'. I carry on checking Facebook, but I am aware that I am checking Facebook. I realise that my breathing is really shallow as it often is when I am using a computer and put my attention on my in and out breaths as I scroll through my newsfeed. I also notice that my shoulders are tight because of the posture I am using with my computer and open them gently and straighten my back while trying to relax.

Get the idea? You can apply these methods on the way to work, while you are at work, especially during breaks. Going to the bathroom or making tea or coffee are great moments to practice Being Present for example. As I said before, travelling is also a good opportunity to practice because there is nothing much else to do when you are on a plane or train or waiting in a queue or departure lounge. Meal times are also a good moment, particularly while washing up.

Using Presence to Help Manage your Psychosis Symptoms (When they are mild!)

Remember, the advice in this guide is not a replacement for the medical treatment that you receive from your doctor. You can use it to help support your recovery. Always follow your doctor's advice! The examples here are for when your symptoms are under control and very mild. If you are in a full blown crisis, you can use these methods to help you, but it is really important to work with your doctor to control your medication and develop these techniques more during your recovery.

Once you have become familiar with the process of Being Present, you can begin to use it to help you when you have unusual thoughts or experiences like hearing voices, or are feeling distressed and paranoid. When you have unusual experiences, it is usually because your Energy is charged up and disordered and your Mind is agitated.

You can use the various ways of Being Present to help you, depending on the situation, and what you find works best.

If you can consciously remember the principle that whatever you are experiencing is your own disordered Energy that has become unintegrated, which is why your experiences like hearing voices appear to be coming from outside, you can already begin to relax a little and embrace the experiences rather than fight with them or try to run away from them.

Hearing Voices I – Noticing and Naming

If you are hearing voices, the very first thing to do is to very simply acknowledge what is happening and say to yourself 'I am hearing voices'. Try not to judge whether hearing voices is good or bad. Try not to get involved in the story of what the voices are saying. Simply notice 'I am hearing voices' and try to relax. Relaxation and insight are really the keys.

Hearing Voices II – Applying Presence to the Body

If noticing and naming your experience with hearing voices followed by relaxing is not helping you, you can try to direct your attention on what you are doing with your body by getting into the here and now.

Whatever you are experiencing, it doesn't matter, just keep bringing yourself back to your body. You can say to yourself, 'I am sitting', 'I am standing up', 'I am walking', 'I am eating', 'I am breathing', 'I am cleaning my house'. You can alternate very strong attention on what you are doing with relaxing. Relaxing is important. You may find that when you fixate on knowing what you are doing with your Body, you stop noticing that you are hearing voices. At this point you can relax and let go of the fixation. If the voices start to return and you feel agitated then you can again start to focus more strongly on what you are doing with your Body, 'I am walking' 'I am sitting', 'I am eating' etc.

Hearing Voices III - Coordinating your Breathing

As I said earlier, having unusual experiences is a result of your Energy level being disordered and one of the best ways to try to help this is to coordinate your breathing. Firstly, you place your attention on your breathing in a relaxed way. If the voices are really strong, you can focus a little more on the sensations of breathing in and breathing out. Once you have placed your attention on your breathing, you can start to coordinate it a little by remaining empty just a little after each out-breath. You breathe in, breathe out and just pause a little. Then breathe in again. Once you get used to this, you can gently extend this pause on the out-breath so that it becomes longer and longer. Remember, it is important never to force anything. Every so often, you can relax and breathe normally without any particular focus. Then, when you become very distracted or agitated again, you can begin again to place your focus on your breathing, pausing at the end of each out-breath.

Hearing Voices IV – Combining the Methods

Once you become more familiar with the above methods and you can apply them fluidly in any given situation, you can also begin to gently combine them. You can name your experience, 'I am hearing voices' and try to relax. Then bring your attention to your body and to whatever it is that you are doing, like walking, sitting, standing, knowing what it is that you are doing and being present with that. At the same time, as you are walking, sitting, eating etc, you can begin to place your attention on your breathing and when you are ready, gently pause on the out-breath, just for a second or two. You don't need to stop what you are doing necessarily in order to be able to do this. It is more a matter of where you prioritise putting your attention. Remember, it is very important to alternate these moments of fixation on what you are doing with relaxation and letting go, otherwise you can make yourself more

◆ ◆ ◆

Paranoia & Delusional Thoughts

Remember the exercise above about noticing and naming thoughts. Well, when you are having paranoid or delusional thoughts, you need to try to get back to the root of what is going on, and that is simply that you are thinking. You need to take your focus away from the content of the thoughts and prioritise noticing and naming them. So for example, if you feel that random people are talking about you and judging you. First, you can try to notice the emotion. 'I am feeling paranoid'. Name it. Then you can also catch your thoughts, like the bear catching salmon above. Whenever a thought arises, catch it, notice it and say to yourself 'I am thinking'. It doesn't matter what the content is, try not to get involved in the story of it. Simply notice that you are thinking and then relax.

This is of course not easy because if you are experiencing these kinds of thoughts, they are probably combined with high levels of confusion and anxiety, which make concentrating difficult. Remember, if your symptoms are too strong, go and see your doctor. Don't struggle by yourself.

The real benefit of becoming familiar with the principles I describe here is to be able to catch things before they go too far.

ABOUT SUICIDAL THOUGHTS

If you are experiencing suicidal thoughts, please tell someone, talk about it and particularly, go and see your doctor. There is no shame in asking for help. If you don't know where to turn, call The Samaritans Tel: 116 123 (UK), or the National Suicide Prevention Helpline Tel: 1-800-273-8255 (USA)

The level of psychological discomfort that we can experience when suffering from psychosis can be extreme and shakes us to our core. It is not like a physical illness where somehow we can step away from it, rationalise it and objectify it to a certain extent. We experience all kinds of delusions, paranoias, persecutory thoughts and hallucinations that are very real for us. As real as anything else with regard to our actual perceptions. For this reason it is logical that many will consider suicide as a 'way out', as an escape from this overwhelming suffering.

I don't want to go too far into this but I do want to say that while this may seem like a 'way out' of suffering, the problem with this logic is that there are in fact no guarantees that this is the case. No matter what anyone says, we actually have no idea what will happen to our consciousness after our physical body passes away. Whatever point of view we adopt, we simply do not actually know for real, and we won't do until we directly have that experience. All that we have are our mental concepts.

If the nihilists among us are correct, then maybe nothing matters, and it doesn't matter at all if we commit suicide or not, but we know that we have an Energy level and that our Energy level is connected with our Mind. Science tells us that energy cannot be destroyed, that it changes and transforms into different states. So on that basis, we can think that there may be some kind of continuation after death even if it is nothing like our current embodied experience. In addition, the actual nature of the Mind and how it functions is not well understood by science and there is no real understanding of what the nature of consciousness actually is, so on this basis, even science does not know what happens after death except on the physical level.

The bottom line here is that suicide may seem like a 'way out' but there is no guarantee at all that this is the case. Things could in fact get a lot worse. Do you really want to take that risk?

Action:

If you are experiencing suicidal thoughts, go and tell your doctor and get some help. Put yourself in their hands. Follow their advice. If you need to talk to someone, call the Samaritans or similar helpline or a trusted friend or family member. At the same time, you can apply the methods of Being Present with thoughts:

When you have a suicidal thought, notice that it is arising. Don't get involved with the story around the thought or the thought itself. Simply catch yourself and notice 'I am thinking' and try to relax. When the thoughts arise again, do it again, catch yourself and notice 'I am thinking' and try to relax.

Don't think of the suicidal thoughts as any different from any other thought. It is not a 'special' thought. It is just a thought.

In addition, you can combine this with using the breathing methods and exercises mentioned above in order to better coordinate and relax your Energy.

TREASURING THE GIFT OF SLEEP

When recovering from psychosis one huge obstacle can be having problems with sleeping. This is an issue that I have had a lot of experience with and it is only recently that I have finally been able to get a handle on managing my sleep more effectively when it goes off track!

When we suffer from sleep problems, we may have difficulty getting to sleep, we may get to sleep ok but then we wake up in the middle of the night and not really get back into deep sleep again, or we may get to sleep but our sleep is very light and we don't feel rested when we get up the next day. Anyone who has suffered from insomnia will know that very often the next day(s) will be a write-off. We can't concentrate, we feel depressed, irritable and angry. Sometimes, we may even feel light headed or dizzy. We use caffeine and other stimulants to wake up and get 'with it', but that charges our Energy and feeds the cycle of insomnia, and in extreme cases this can all spiral out of control and we may go for days or even weeks and months without sleeping well.

Sleep deprivation itself can be a major cause of psychosis, so we can see how important it is that we find ways to sleep well in order to protect our mental health. We need to learn to value our sleep and to Be Present with the habits we have around sleeping in order to get on top of this. Sleep is a treasure that we need to guard and protect. If we sleep well, everything else in our life will go much more smoothly. It is fundamental.

Causes of Insomnia

Here are some of the main causes of insomnia:

Anxiety: Anxiety is a major cause of insomnia and insomnia is a major cause of anxiety. Anxiety feeds insomnia and the bad feelings one has as a result of the insomnia feeds the anxiety and leads to poorer sleep.

It can seem a bit like a chicken and egg situation to try to find which one came first, so it needs to be addressed from all angles. See the section on overcoming anxiety for help with that and read on for more direct help with your sleep. Most likely though, the anxiety arrived before the insomnia did.

Stress: We live in a busy and complicated world. It is hard to avoid stress completely but we can be aware of stress and try to learn how to manage it. On the other hand, we need a certain level of stress in our lives because it provides drive and motivation and spurs us into action. This is part of our natural life, but when it goes too far, it can start to upset the balance of our Energy.

The hormones such as cortisol that are released into our systems when we are stressed inhibit our ability to sleep well and good sleep helps us to recover from the negative effects of stress.

Diet & Lifestyle: In Tibetan medicine, there is a very developed language for describing mental disturbances related to insomnia through the concept of *'Lung'*. *Lung* in Tibetan medicine is a kind of internal 'Wind' and relates to the Prana energy found in the various systems of Yoga. There are various 'Winds' that provide different active functions in the body such as digestion or immunity. '*Lung*' is also very much related with the function of the Mind. If the '*Lung*' is balanced and flowing correctly, then the Mind will be calm and peaceful. If it is not flowing correctly, the Mind will be disturbed.

There is a section on diet later in this guide but it is useful to know with regard to insomnia that there are certain foods and activities that can agitate the '*Lung*' and others that can calm it down.

Poor Sleep Hygiene: Sleep hygiene is all of the things that we do in the 90 minutes before going to sleep. Basically, if we overstimulate ourselves before we go to bed by thinking about work, using computers and smartphones or watching movies etc, it can adversely affect the quality of our sleep.

We can think of insomnia as being an expression of disordered 'Energy' which either has a physical cause related with our Body, or a mental / emotional cause related with our Mind. Whatever the origin, our Energy becomes disordered and it affects our ability to sleep. Once our Energy has become disordered, we need to find a way to coordinate it and we need to approach that from all angles.

Good Sleep Toolkit

I came across a book called 'Sleep' by Nick Littlehales who works with top athletes to maximise the effectiveness of their sleep in order to increase their performance. I found the methods in his book very easy to use and very effective and will summarise some of the things that I found most useful here along with a few other tips that I have picked up along the way. I strongly recommend that you read his book if you want to learn more. Also, I found that the process of empowering myself through education about sleep actually helped to reduce my insomnia and to reduce my anxiety around it. This is another example of how not being passive can be really positive. For a long time I felt like a victim of my poor sleep and didn't have the inspiration, energy or motivation to inform myself about it and find a way to get on top of it so I remained passive and the problem persistedConsistent Wake Up Time: Choose a wake up time that will be the same every single day. Stick to it as much as you can, even if you feel like you need to lie in and 'catch up' on sleep. This is the key to everything that follows.

Measuring 90 Minute Sleep Cycles: A sleep cycle is 90 minutes on average. This means the time that it takes to descend into sleep, enter deep sleep, come out of deep sleep, then become conscious and descend into sleep again. On average, we will have about five 90 minute cycles of sleep per night (7.5 hrs).

You should start to measure everything in 90 minute cycles from your chosen wakeup time and only go to sleep, or have afternoon or evening naps at the start of each of these 90 minute time slots. The point is to habituate your body to these 90 minute cycles.

For example, my personal wakeup time is 7:30am. The sleep that I need is usually 5 cycles but can also be 4 cycles. I therefore need to go to bed at 12:00am in order to get up at 7:30am to get 5 cycles or go to bed at 1:30am to get 4 cycles. I might have a nap in the afternoon at 3:00pm or 4:30pm, but could also have a nap at 6:00pm for example.

Quality, Not Quantity: The next thing to do is find out how much sleep that you personally actually need. I have discovered for myself that it is much better to go to bed later and have a shorter, better quality sleep than go to bed earlier and have a lighter, poorer quality sleep. Just because 7.5 hrs is the average does not mean that there is no variation to this number, so discover for yourself how much sleep you actually need.

8 Hours Per Day - **35 Cycles Per Week – Napping Allowed:** Culturally we are very attached to the 8 hrs per day model of sleep. This is what we think and are told that we should all be getting in order to be healthy.

Instead, we should first look at how much sleep we actually need as this may vary from person to person. Then, instead of thinking in terms of hours per day, we should think in terms of 90 minute cycles per week. This gives us the freedom to add cycles throughout the day and evening if we have the possibility and helps to remove the anxiety we can have around getting our '8 hrs per night' all in one go.

The Minimalist Bedroom: Creating a good environment in which to sleep is very important. Your curtains should be blackout curtains that do not let in any light. The lighting should be warm. Your bedroom environment should be as decluttered as humanly possible. Put stuff away in drawers, out of sight. You don't want to be visually stimulated by anything before going to sleep. If at all possible, only use your bedroom for sleeping and nothing else. That means no TV and especially no smartphones or laptops!

The Sacred 90 Minutes Before Bedtime: It is useful to think that throughout most of our evolutionary history, we did not have electricity and the level of complex mental stimulation that we have now. When it became dark, we would have gathered around a fire and only engaged in activities that one can do in firelight. We would not have been sparking our fight or flight systems by watching the news, streaming TV shows, browsing the web or playing video games.

If we adopt this understanding in the 90 minutes before we go to sleep, it can help a lot. Turn off all bright lights, use soft, warm lighting or candles. Don't engage in stimulating activities. Maybe do some simple, calming mundane stuff like ironing or washing up.

Avoid screen time. The blue light from computer and mobile device screens can actually inhibit the release of melatonin in your body which is the hormone that makes us feel sleepy and helps us to go to sleep and have good quality sleep once we are there.

Reading is good, storytelling around the fire is allowed! But be careful what type of story you choose. It should be relaxing, not taxing. Try to use an actual book that is made from paper.

To Sleep or Not to Sleep... with a Partner: If you have a partner and you have problems sleeping, it is much better to sleep in separate beds, or on opposite sides of a huge bed. This can be difficult for some partners to accept because they can feel like it is an indication that you don't love them or want to be with them but it really is not like that at all and you need to find a way to communicate very well about this and come to a mutual understanding. You shouldn't have to apologise for this. It is your health. If intimacy at the time of sleep means that one of you gets '8 hours' of sleep and the other is lying in bed staring at the ceiling all night and feeling like dirt the next day, it is much better to come to another arrangement, not only for your personal health but the health of your relationship too.

Caffeine: If you are currently having problems with sleep, you need to do   everything you can to calm your Energy down and stabilise it so that peaks and troughs are minimised. In that way, you hold less tension and find it easier to have a more restful sleep. As we all know, caffeine (found in coffee, tea, chocolate, mate, cola, energy drinks etc) is a stimulant and has the effect of charging our energy in order to give us a temporary boost. It is very tempting to use caffeine when we are going through a bout of insomnia because we feel like it helps us to get going and do the things that we need to throughout the day and to some extent this is true. But when your insomnia is severe, it is best to avoid caffeine altogether in order to stabilise your Energy.

If your insomnia is mild then limit your caffeine intake to the mornings. The thing to remember is that it takes 10-12hrs for caffeine to leave your body so ideally if you use caffeine, you should do it 10-12hrs before your bedtime.

Avoiding Sugar and Comfort Eating: I love sugar and have a terrible sweet tooth, so it pains me to say SUGAR IS BADDDD. I severely limited my use of refined sugar products recently (anything that has additional sugar added to it) and guess what: I survived! Now, I am astonished when I walk into a supermarket and see it with new eyes, realising that probably more than 50% of the stuff in there is not actually food. They are peddling drugs in the form of sugar based products. There are rows and rows of sweets, sugary drinks, cakes etc, none of which is the actual nutrition that we need.

Sugar in a similar way to caffeine, gives us the feeling of a temporary energy boost. Our sugar 'high' is then followed by a sugar 'low' which can then lead to a highly addictive sugar consumption cycle (which whole industries are built on!). When we feel terrible after a night of insomnia, it can be tempting to use sugar to give ourselves a lift, but again, this is destabilising for our Energy. It is encouraging peaks and troughs rather than a smooth constant flow. For this reason (apart from all of the other negative health implications of consuming sugar), I recommend avoiding adding any kind of refined sugar to your diet. Just to be very clear, that means any product that has sugar in its list of ingredients should be avoided!

Another thing to remember is that all carbohydrates are sugars too. That means bread, croissants, pasta, rice, potatoes etc, which is why we love them so much. A typical pasta dish for example is probably 80-90% carbs. I don't recommend eating meals with more than 50% carbs. I also recommend avoiding eating too many of these things in their refined forms. Try to use wholefood options.

Comfort eating is something to be aware of and to avoid if possible. Comfort eating is basically eating when we are not actually hungry between our regular mealtimes, and or over eating at mealtimes. It is very easy to comfort eat when we suffer from insomnia because we feel awful, and in order not to feel this way, we look for the closest and easiest ways of not feeling the way we feel. When we have that extra slice of toast, that extra big serving of pasta, we reach for the biscuits, we are masking the way that we feel. There is something childlike about comfort eating, as if we are an infant being soothed by our mothers milk. Temporarily this may be true, but there is a cost.

The problem is that comfort eating can lead us to become overweight, less physically active and mentally more passive so it is better to first be aware of the habit of comfort eating and then try to think of some replacement foods and behaviours. For example, instead of reaching for the biscuit tin or that slice of toast, eat a carrot with some tahini or peanut butter on it, or an apple. Drink a lot more water. Take yourself out for walks or do some other type of exercise.

Extreme Insomnia: When your insomnia is extreme, it may be time to ask your doctor for some sleeping medication in the short term.

On a medium to long term basis, we need to be aware of the fact that we can become resistant to the drugs and they become less effective over time. Sleeping pills can also become addictive if taken for too long, so we need a longer term approach that is that will move us away from needing to rely on medication.

What I suggest is that you implement the methods that I have described above during the period that you take your prescribed sleeping pills. By the time you come off your sleeping pills, you will already have your new sleep routine in place.

IDENTIFYING YOUR PSYCHOSIS TRIGGERS

Throughout your recovery process, there will be certain people, places, thought patterns, habitual patterns, associations and stimuli that will tend to trigger your symptoms and make you fearful of slipping back into the psychotic state. When you find yourself exposed to these things, you will begin to feel more edgy, more anxious, more wobbly.

One of the reasons that it is good to catch and treat psychosis as early as possible is that treatment with medication can be effective in calming the symptoms down, but it cannot erase the memories of your psychotic experiences which, for you at the time of experiencing them, appeared to be real. Therefore, when you find yourself in certain situations you can experience 'flashbacks' or memories of your psychosis. Obviously the fewer memories you have of that, the better!

At the beginning of your recovery process, it is important to make a kind of map of the things that can trigger you to feel unstable and think of some strategies that you can put in place to overcome them. This is about understanding the territory that you are working with and preparing yourself so that you are less likely to be taken by surprise and knocked backwards. Obvious examples of things that may trigger you to feel wobbly may be hangovers from alcohol use, lack of sleep, or being in loud, busy social situations. Your triggers may also be certain emotions or thought patterns. All of us will have our own set of unique triggers and it is up to us to be active in noticing what they are.

Social situations can be very challenging if you have suffered from psychosis, because you know what you have been through and it can be easy to think that it is very obvious to other people too. You can feel like you are walking around with a big fluorescent sticker on your forehead that says 'I have mental health problems'. It can make you feel very insecure around other people, especially if you know that they know what you have been through. This is a kind of self-conditioning that it is important to be aware of and to try to relax with, otherwise, you are in danger of adopting the identity of 'someone with mental health problems' which can become a limitation to your recovery. You can literally block your progress by putting yourself in the box of being 'unwell'. Also, if you put yourself in that box, you are unconsciously inviting other people to do the same.

The fact is that most people are totally wrapped up in their own problems and their own lives and no one really cares what is going on with you unless it directly affects them personally, so if you feel nervous and neurotic around other people, just try to relax. In most cases you will realise after a while that your fears are unfounded. This will give you confidence.

In any case, if you feel like a particular situation is too much for you and you don't feel like you have any tools to deal with it, don't worry, be patient, be kind to yourself, like a kind mother, just take yourself away from that situation the best way that you can and avoid exposing yourself to it again until you feel stronger and more able to cope. There may also be certain things, people and places that you simply decide that you no longer need in your life and you just let them go.

Action:

Begin to make a list of all of the things that tend to trigger you into feeling wobbly, anxious and unstable. You can write down the obvious things first and then throughout the coming days and weeks make a note of all or the more subtle things that come up. For the more troublesome triggers, you can do a bit of analysis using some simple Cognitive Behavioural Therapy (CBT) techniques:

Make a flowchart or spider diagram to help you that includes the trigger, what it makes makes you feel, physically and mentally, and what actions or behaviours it leads you into doing. Then you can make an analysis – is there logic to the trigger and your response to it? If so, what is it? Then you can come up with a solution of how to work with the trigger and your responses to it. You may find that the clarity that you gain from doing this analysis alone will be a big step towards overcoming your trigger.

If there is a logic to why you are being triggered then you can think of ways to overcome or avoid the problem. For example if you are suffering from insomnia and this directly affects or mental stability, it is very important to try to find ways to sleep better (see the section on sleep above).

If there is no logic, you can try to generate some logic and reasoning to help yourself to relax as a kind of antidote. For example, you don't like walking into cafes or bars because they make you feel paranoid and think that everyone is looking at you and judging you (Trigger). In this case, you can do a kind of analysis by asking some questions to yourself like 'how does this make me feel?'. You can list the feelings that come up. Then you can observe what actions these thoughts and feelings lead you to take, like withdrawing and not talking to anyone, or leaving, or getting drunk, or overeating. Then you do a kind of analysis of the situation; Do I know any of these people? If not, then why would I care what they think of me? What makes me think that they are even noticing me at all? What evidence do I have that this is the case? Even if you do know those people, what evidence do you have that what they are talking about has anything to do with you? Why would you care anyway?

SEXUAL ENERGY
& PSYCHOSIS

Because the onset of my own psychosis came on during my teens, it seemed very connected with the development of my sexual energy. Puberty, and navigating the new terrain of being a sexually activated person is an anxiety inducing time for any child or young adult and I grew up in an environment where there was a lot of repression and shame around sex, especially when my two brothers and I were very young, although things did get a bit more relaxed later on. My parents were of a generation where mostly, 'one doesn't talk about sex', or one's feelings and emotions in general, or relationships and their dynamics and complexities. All of it was pretty much off the menu when we were young.

My dad used to freak out if anything sexual came onto the TV making comments like 'I don't want to see this filth on my TV'. In my opinion, this was very damaging because it communicated that sex is bad and shameful, something to be hidden away or concealed. My Mum was more open minded, but Dad was the one who dominated the atmosphere in the house in that regard because he was volatile and we were all scared of his temper. My dad at that time was also strongly conditioned by religious beliefs about sex before marriage and even masturbation being shameful.

My parents seemed to me to be very fearful about sex in relation to us children, that we may get someone pregnant (I have two brothers), and at the same moment, the extent of the AIDS epidemic was beginning to emerge in the media (it was in the 90's) and there was a lot of fear around HIV and AIDS. But rather than creating an atmosphere of dialogue and expression, the whole subject was taboo. It was always something hidden away, there was no atmosphere of encouragement to explore relationships. We never had a conversation like '...that's great that you have a girlfriend. I am really happy for you. I am here for you if you ever need to talk about anything'. It was more like 'is that a good idea?' or forbidding us to meet people saying 'you are much too young'.

At the same time, my inner experience of sexual energy in that moment was that the sheer power of it was at times overwhelming and intoxicating. It was a bit like those videos you see of people learning to ride motorbikes where they have no idea of the power of the accelerator and end up pulling unintentional wheelies and doing backflips, or zigzagging wildly across the road and falling off.

The immense power of this energy made me feel ashamed especially when it became connected with an actual partner! I had no idea how to behave. I craved intimacy but found it impossible to be myself and to relax. I was not a secure teen and the dissonance between the need of my outer teenage self to pretend that everything is cool and that I knew everything, and my inner teenage self who felt totally out of control and out of my depth was hard to live with and I began to become knotted up inside. This strongly dualistic tension accumulated over time and I am sure that it fed into my later psychosis.

I think that all of this would have been a lot easier if there had been a much greater atmosphere of openness and communication around sex and relationships in my family and also in school. A 'sex positive' environment. I had received no tools whatsoever from my early experiences to manage my growth into a sexual being, only a sense of shame and concealment in relation to my parents and competition in relation to my brothers and friends.

There was no culture of supportive dialogue around sex, or sharing worries, doubts or even sharing good experiences. There were no open doors. I think if there had been, we would have all been much more relaxed with the process. I wouldn't have ended up being so neurotic and intimacy would not have become such a strong trigger.

These days, there appears to be a much more open culture of dialogue and understanding about sex and relationships in families and schools and I am sure that creating this kind of atmosphere is very beneficial for children and teens to be able to have more healthy relationships in their adult lives.

Action:

If you can relate to the points that I have made in this section, I recommend that you explore your relationship to your sexual energy with a counsellor or psychotherapist in order to try to understand more deeply what is going on with you. If this is not possible, do some reading and exploring for yourself by reading books about sex and sexuality.

One thing that was absolutely absent in my life until even quite recently was any education about how relationships and attraction work. This is a big gaping hole in our education and we all more or less go into the world of relationships having to work things out for ourselves through trial and error. Fortunately there are a huge number of useful resources online and in books that can help us to understand these things better and make better informed choices. I have also included a small section on relationships and intimacy below.

BEING CAREFUL
WITH SELF TALK

*What Scripts and Narratives
are Running in your Head?*

O ne way to work with thoughts is to simply Be Present with them as mentioned above, by noticing that you are thinking and then relaxing. But sometimes, it can be useful to dig into them a little and analyse them in a more intellectual way if they are repetitive thoughts that you feel like are conditioning you. As I mentioned above, 'you are what you eat'. You can also apply this to your thought processes and discover that 'you become what you tell yourself you are'. It is probably worth mentioning this again here because it is important to keep an eye on your 'self-talk'.

Everyone has a self reflective script or narrative that plays out in their minds which can be conscious or unconscious, the content of which will depend a lot on their previous experiences and their levels of security or insecurity. The thing is that we often don't question these narratives because they can be quite fleeting in the moment, and they pass away quickly, and like dreams, we can forget them quickly. Why should we be aware of this? Because our internal dialogue can condition us and this can be negative if our internal dialogue is undermining our security.

For example, if we call or message someone and they don't call us back in a time frame that we expect. Someone with a healthy and secure internal narrative will think to themselves something like 'oh they must be busy'. Someone with a less healthy, less secure internal narrative may say to themselves something like 'this person doesn't like me', 'I must have done something wrong', 'I am not good enough, that is why they haven't answered'.

Action:

Write a list of all the negative self talk phrases that go through your Mind as they come up. It is useful to have a notebook for these kinds of things that you can carry around with you, or a notes app on a smartphone. You will notice that some of these thoughts are quite vague and fleeting, but some are stronger and deeper and are influencing you quite a lot. For the stronger and deeper thoughts, it can be useful to catch them and challenge them using a similar analysis to that which we did above on identifying psychosis triggers.

Examples:

Thought Pattern: I am not good enough

What it Makes You Feel: Frustrated, ashamed, lacking in confidence

Challenge: I am not good enough at what? (break it down, be specific). Why do I feel I am not good enough? What steps can I take in order to progress in this specific area?

❖ ❖ ❖

Thought Pattern: Everybody hates me

What it Makes You Feel: Neurotic, self conscious, lacking in confidence

Challenge: Who hates me? Be specific. Is it true? If so, why? Is there anything I can do about it? If I have a problem with one person, does that mean I have a problem with everyone? Is it helpful to generalise in this way? List all the friends and family who you know care about you. Are you pushing them away with your own anger?

❖ ❖ ❖

Thought Pattern: I'll never be successful

What it Makes You Feel: Fearful, hesitant, lacking in confidence, ashamed

Challenge: Is it helpful to generalise in this way? Successful at what? (be specific, break it down). Are your expectations of yourself reasonable? Are there steps that you can take in order to move towards success in this given area? List all of your past successes, no matter how small. Ask yourself what success actually means to you personally.

❖ ❖ ❖

Thought Pattern: I am a lost cause

What it Makes You Feel: Hopeless, lethargic, difficulty in making decisions

Challenge: Again, is it helpful to generalise in this way? A lost cause in what respect? In what area of your life? (break it down). Maybe some things have not worked out for you in the past, but does this mean you are always a lost cause? There is always room to develop and progress. Think of how you may be able to do this.

◆ ◆ ◆

Thought Pattern: I am not lovable

What it Makes You Feel: Lonely, angry, jealous, isolated, shy, resentful, depressed

Challenge: Again, is it helpful to generalise in this way? Think of the times when you have been loved and loving. Did you feel like you were not lovable then? Maybe it would be helpful to think instead 'in this moment I feel lonely and unlovable, what steps can I take to connect with other people?'

◆ ◆ ◆

Notice that all of the above negative thought patterns are very generalised statements. 'I am not good enough' for example. By allowing statements like this to float around in our Minds unchecked, we are allowing them to fix us into a position. We are conditioned on some level by the statement and that affects our behaviour and how we interact in the world.

A useful trick here is to remember that everything is relative and impermanent. There is not a single thing that arises without causes and conditions that contribute to their creation. If we understand what these causes and conditions are, these thought patterns will have less power over us. What we need to do is to transform these thoughts from statements into something more relative, temporal and fluid.

For example:

> 'I don't feel in this moment like I am good enough, because...'

> 'I feel in this moment like everybody hates me, because...'

> 'I feel in this moment like I will never be successful, because...'

> 'I feel in this moment like I am a lost cause, because...'

> 'I feel in this moment like I am not lovable, because...'

You see the difference? These statements have a very different flavour, they are fluid, they show an understanding of the causes, of the fact that they are momentary in time and they imply that because you understand the cause, there can be a solution. How do you understand the causes? By asking questions.

'Why don't I feel good enough?' 'Good enough in relation to what?' 'Is this legitimate or am I exaggerating?' 'Is there something I can do in order to feel good enough?' 'If so, what steps do I need to take in order to do that?', or 'do I simply have unrealistic expectations that I need to let go of?'

TALKING THERAPIES

T alking therapies are incredibly useful and I cannot recommend finding a qualified Counsellor, Cognitive Behavioural Therapy (CBT) practitioner or Psychotherapist enough. Why?

Suffering from psychosis, or any mental illness for that matter can be very isolating. You can feel totally alone with your experiences and your friends and family are very unlikely to have the skills necessary to be present for you, or to help you effectively. It is possible that they may actually, without meaning to, make things worse.

A qualified therapist will be someone totally outside of your immediate social circle that you will see regularly. They will form part of your 'scaffolding' as you rebuild your confidence and self esteem. They will be someone who is trained to hold a space in which you can be yourself, who will not judge you, but who will skilfully encourage you to share your experiences, hopes and fears and who will act as a kind of mirror to help you understand what is going on. Depending on the type of therapy it is, they may also give you exercises and techniques that will help you to manage your symptoms should they arise.

I strongly recommend that you ask your healthcare service to provide you with counselling therapy as soon as you possibly can, for as long as it is possible if it is available. Some healthcare systems will offer it as part of their treatment program, particularly Cognitive Behavioural Therapy (CBT) which is proven to help with the treatment of psychosis along with depression and anxiety.

If you are able to fund it, I recommend that you find a therapist privately and develop a long term therapeutic relationship with them. If money is an issue, which it often is, many therapy schools run student clinics at very low cost in order to train their students. Some therapists also offer low cost solutions for people on low incomes. This can be a good option to get you started.

You may think to yourself 'wow, therapy is so expensive, I can't afford it!' and it is true, it can be expensive, but you can also ask yourself 'can I afford not to do this?'. A therapist can save you a lot of time where you may be floundering around in the dark. The sooner you get back on your feet, the more effective you will be, and the more likely you will be able to generate the resources that you need in order to have the kind of lifestyle that you want and deserve.

Cognitive Behavioural Therapy (CBT)

CBT is the standard therapy offered by medical professionals in order to support recovery from psychosis, along with medication. CBT provides you with a set of tools in order to help you to visualise and understand what is going on when you are having difficulties. This helps you to look at the types of thoughts you are having, the feelings associated with them, the physical sensations that can accompany the thoughts, and the behaviours that these lead to. Once you understand how the process works, you can work with your therapist to find ways to reverse the negative thought, feeling, sensation, behaviour cycle into a positive one.

For example, you may have thoughts like 'I always mess things up' or 'Nobody likes me'. Those thoughts lead you to feelings of sadness, self consciousness or anxiety. When you think or feel like that, it can affect your behaviour, making you withdraw from others or stop doing the things that you enjoy. Physically, you may feel tense, suffer from palpitations or have low energy. Any one of these thoughts, feelings, behaviours or body sensations can lead to the generation of the others so that self fulfilling negative feedback loop is created.

You will work with your CBT therapist to look at the negative cycle and try to find which elements you can change in order to reverse the cycle from a negative loop into a positive one. A simplistic example related to the example above would be, instead of 'withdrawing from others', making a point of socialising more, which in turn will help us to feel more energised, less sad and as a result, we will feel like we have friends and that people like us, which will make us want to socialise more.

Another CBT method is to encourage us to ask relevant questions about why we may think, feel or behave a certain way. For example the thought 'nobody likes me', which leads to feeling sad, having no energy and withdrawing from others which can make us feel even more like 'nobody likes me', so the cycle continues. In CBT, we will break this down into small, easily digestible parts. For example:

'Why do I feel that nobody likes me?' Are there concrete reasons, Yes or No?

If yes, what are they?

What evidence do I have that this is true? Is there something in my behaviour that is making this happen like being rude or aggressive? Is there something that I can do about it?

If the answer is that there are no concrete reasons why we feel that way, we can think about how it is not helping us to allow this thought to condition us and try to let it go instead, perhaps replacing the thought with another that says 'of course people like me!' We could also approach this through our behaviour by socialising more, in which case we may find that actually people do like us when we interact with them which will reduce our thoughts that 'nobody likes me' and start a positive cycle.

Of course every situation is different and when you are in the middle of something, it can be very difficult to step outside of it and see it objectively. This is why it is very useful to work with a therapist because they will have an objective view and will be able to point out things to you that you may not be able to see for yourself. If you do not have the possibility to work with a therapist, there are many resources online that can help you to learn some of the tools of CBT with worksheets and other tools that can help you.

Limitations of CBT

CBT is an awesome toolbox of helpful methods and principles that you can learn and use with a qualified therapist and also, later, take away with you and use as part of your personal mental health care regime. A bit like a skincare regime but for your Mind. What CBT will help you most with is your present condition. You will address challenging thoughts, emotions and anxieties that you are experiencing now and learn ways that you can manage them, and for many of us, that is all we will need and want.

Where CBT appears more limited is in discovering what the origins of those difficult thoughts, emotions and anxieties are. You may discover some of these things through your use of CBT, but with certain types of challenging and damaging patterns, this can be a little like trimming the leaves and branches from a plant in order to keep it under control. What you really need to do is pull it out by the roots if it is causing too much of a problem.

If we understand the real causes of challenging patterns, it is possible that we can overcome them in a much more profound and embodied way. For this reason, other types of therapy such as psychotherapy and certain types of counselling may help you more as they will go deeper into your inner experience. Using these therapies you will explore your current challenges and look at how they are shaped and formed by your early relationships and experiences. Very often the problems we have are rooted in our early childhood experiences and these are very difficult for us to unravel by ourselves because our childhood experiences form the fabric of who we feel we are and it is difficult for us to step outside of that without objective help from a qualified therapist. It can also be a very long process, one that requires some patience, effort and commitment on your part, but the rewards can be great.

Counselling and Psychotherapy

In counselling and psychotherapy, your therapist, when you find one who you feel comfortable with, will be there for you through thick and thin and they will be someone who you will have provided for yourself, a gift that you have given yourself. You will do most of the work, discovering and nurturing the parts of you that are wounded. Your therapist will hold a safe space for you to do that and gently nudge you to help you to understand yourself better and the causes of your distress. Once you understand the causes of problems, it is much easier to find solutions in order to overcome them, or at least to accept and live with them!

There is also something about the consistent nature of this kind of therapeutic relationship that can provide a deep sense of security that may otherwise have been missing in your life. You may also find that rather than lean on your friends and family for therapeutic support, you are able to rely on your therapist instead which will allow your other relationships to be much more healthy and less dependent.

How Can I Find a Good Therapist?

When you start looking into finding a therapist, especially a counsellor or psychotherapist, it can be very confusing as there are so many different types of psychotherapy and counselling schools, it is hard to know where to start. With CBT, it is easier because CBT is CBT and it is more a case of finding someone that you feel comfortable with.

I suggest at first, trying to find out if anyone that you know and who you respect is seeing a therapist and ask them if they would recommend them to you and introduce you to them. If it is appropriate, their therapist may be able to see you for treatments themselves. If that is not appropriate or possible, they will be able to refer you to one of their trusted colleagues. Therapists will not see you if your relationship with their existing client is too close or intertwined as it would affect their objectivity in their existing therapeutic relationship, so don't take any rejection on this basis personally. You will be able to confidently follow their referral to a trusted colleague.

If you cannot get a recommendation from a friend, then you need to go through the professional therapist associations in your country. Anyone who is a member of one of these organisations will have had extensive training over several years and will have accumulated a significant amount of supervised clinical hours. They will also be committed to following a strict code of ethical conduct and to continue their professional training for a minimum amount of hours per year throughout their professional careers. In the UK, the main accreditation bodies are UKCP (for Counselling and Psychotherapy), the BACP (for Counselling and Psychotherapy), BABCP (for Cognitive Behavioural Therapy). Anyone who is a member of these organisations is qualified to help you.

When you contact a therapist, it is normal to go and have an initial meeting with them for you to assess each other. This process is quite subjective, and for both you and the therapist, you will need to follow your guts somewhat. Do you feel like you can relate to this person? Sometimes, like anyone you may meet, you might just not get along, in which case it is better not to start the therapy and to keep looking until you find someone that you feel comfortable with.

There are different flavours of therapy and it is quite confusing to know which one may be best for you. Whichever one you choose, I recommend committing yourself to getting the most out of it. Try not to miss sessions, try to be open and receptive both to yourself and to your therapist. Be willing to feel uncomfortable feelings deeply in your being and to explore them. Engage and take responsibility for your process. Don't be passive and expect the therapist to 'do it for you'. They are there to help you to help yourself. You have to be brave in order to go through therapy because it can challenge everything that you think you know about yourself. The reward of going through this process is that you can learn to inhabit your authentic self in a much more real way. You will have a much stronger sense of who you are at your core, not just as an intellectual idea but as a deep authentic presence. You will also have much more capacity to process and filter the challenges that the world throws at you.

UK Professional Therapist Associations

Each of the associations below have websites with 'find a therapist' pages where you can search for a qualified therapist in your area.

British Association for Behavioural and Cognitive Psychotherapies. BABCP (Cognitive Behavioural Therapy)

UK Council for Psychotherapy
UKCP (Counselling & Psychotherapy)

British Association for Counselling and Psychotherapy
BACP (Counselling & Psychotherapy)

PRACTICAL RECOVERY GUIDE - PART III

Getting Back on your Feet

EVERY SHIP NEEDS
A RUDDER

Setting Goals and Creating Purpose

Setting some goals at this point can really help you to develop clarity and direction in your life. Without goals, you are in danger of drifting aimlessly around like a boat without a rudder. If you want to go on a journey, you first need to have some idea of where it is that you want to go and then make some kind of plan about the steps you will need to take in order to get there. You can think of your ability to achieve goals as being a bit like training muscles. You can start by getting into the habit of setting short term goals and achieving them which gives you confidence and makes you stronger. Then you can introduce your long term goals as you become more confident.

Action:

Starting Small – Setting Short Term Goals

Remember, you should never push too hard and you should always do things in a relaxed way. So at first, you can keep it simple and just make a goal for your day. A good way to do this is to think about it the evening before. 'Tomorrow, as well as my usual routine, my goal is to do 30 minutes of stretching or Yoga' for example, or 'Tomorrow, I will do my weekly shopping', or 'Tomorrow, I will spend an hour re-searching local volunteering opportunities'. The point here is to make a plan, no matter how small and execute it. Then, feel the satisfaction of having created a goal and fulfilled it. As each day goes by and each small goal is completed, your confidence and self esteem will grow and develop in a very satisfying way.

As you begin to feel better, you can prepare more ambitious and complex goals for longer periods of time such as a goal for your week. For example, 'this week I want to enrol in and take my first Yoga class' or a goal for your month like 'this month I want to go to my Yoga class once per week and have practiced by myself at home at least twice every week for a month'

The more you do this, the more confidence and clarity you will develop.

Rebuilding Confidence and Self Esteem

There is no doubt about it that suffering from psychosis can damage your confidence and self esteem hugely. There are taboos as a result of ignorance around mental health which can lead to feelings of shame. There can also be a tendency to simply brush it under the carpet and pretend that it never happened, to 'keep your chin up and move on'. This kind of attitude appears strong, but it is brittle and can break easily. It is much better to open the conversation about mental health, to develop a common language around it, to familiarise ourselves with it. To acknowledge what has happened to us, to respect it along with our limitations.

You may feel like you are damaged goods, that you are broken, that you will never be good enough or 'normal' again. I still struggle with this at times and am still on this journey myself, but I can say that it gets better with time and experience and I can share some of the things that have worked for me so far.

Volunteering

> *If you want happiness for an hour, take a nap. If you want happiness for a day, go fishing. If you want happiness for a year, inherit a fortune. If you want happiness for a lifetime, help someone else.*

> Chinese Proverb

When I was a child, I had a moment where I felt extremely unhappy. In our house, there was a small Chinese statue of a fat, laughing man made of wood that my grandfather had given to my mother. The story was that you should rub the belly of this little figure and make a wish. I felt so desperate at this point that I rubbed the belly of this statue and wished very strongly to be happy, but at a certain moment I had the thought that I am not the only person in the world who may be feeling bad. If my wish to become happy comes true, can it be real happiness if I know that there are other people suffering just like I am, or maybe worse? I then changed my wish to make it into one where I wished for all beings to be happy including myself, and that felt better!

The only way, in my opinion, to rebuild confidence and self esteem is through generating new positive experiences and one of the best ways to generate positive experiences is to do something useful for others.

We cannot sit in our house or room and think ourselves into having confidence and self esteem. We gradually need to go out there and make new connections, forge new relationships, gain new skills and experiences that help us to understand that we are not broken, that we do have value and qualities and skills to offer the world. One excellent way to do this is through volunteering.

There are many diverse opportunities for volunteering in many countries around the world. Becoming a volunteer is generally less pressured than getting a contracted job. You will usually be able to choose how much or how little you wish to work and because voluntary organisations really need volunteers, you won't have too much problem of being filtered out by application processes depending on the role. Even if you already have a successful career and qualifications, volunteering can be a great way to get you back on your feet. You can go and help out in an inner city soup kitchen, help clearing footpaths in the countryside, work in a charity shop, do care work, provide company for isolated people. The possibilities are endless, just do a web search for volunteering in your area and I am sure you will find many opportunities.

Why is volunteering useful for you? Well, you get to connect with other people and interact with them in a practical way based around a shared activity within a pre-established frame of reference. This can be a lot less complicated than connecting with people in purely social ways and can lead to building concrete, long lasting friendships and connections. You are also doing practical stuff while volunteering that is useful for others, which gives a sense of fulfilment and takes you out of yourself and your own personal story for a time. Depending on what type of volunteering you do, you may pick up new skills that you can bring forward into a future job. You can also add any volunteering experience that you gain to your CV and acquire references from the organisation that you volunteer with, which will increase your chances of being employed later.

Internships

An internship is an arrangement that you come to with an employer where you basically work with them for free, or on an expenses only basis. Like volunteering, it can be a great way to gain experience and the kind of experience that you gain will quite possibly much more specific than it would be if you were doing voluntary work, and more relevant to a future career path that you may wish to pursue. Possible internships are advertised on many job search websites. You could also consider approaching specific employers directly if you are interested in working for them.

Getting Paid Work – Avoiding the Dependency Trap

After suffering a psychotic episode, you may find yourself on state benefits because you will be unable to work. Or you may become dependent on the support of family or friends. This is great, for a while if you have that possibility because it gives you some breathing space to get yourself together, especially if you follow the advice in this guide. But...

Be careful of relying on state benefits or generous family and friends for too long! If you become too dependent on this kind of support, you can become passive, and as we have already said, to be passive is not a positive state. You can become vulnerable to negativity - negative attitudes and disempowering self beliefs, so it is good to be aware of this from the start. Okay, if you are receiving support from benefits or others while developing yourself through voluntary work or education, this is fine, but there is something rewarding and beneficial for your self esteem if you can find a way to become financially independent, to pay your own bills, to make some effort in a working environment and to be rewarded for it.

Of course, finding work is not always so easy and the world that we live in these days is uncertain in this regard, but it is good to be aware of the pitfalls of relying on benefits and the support of others. Some people enter into the benefits culture in particular as a kind of lifestyle choice because in certain cases they will be worse off if they get a job than they would be on benefits. This may seem logical, but there is a tradeoff in that it is difficult to feel like you are progressing in life if you do this and it is important to feel like you are making progress in some sort of direction in order to feel fulfilled. As I said above, using voluntary work as a stepping stone into paid work can be a great way forward if you do not have a career or qualifications at this time.

Overcoming Social Anxiety

One of the areas which can be really strongly affected by an episode of psychosis can be social confidence. During your delusional psychotic state, you may have experienced other people as part of some huge conspiracy against you, some other-worldly beings who may have been tormenting you. Now that you are 'back', you find that you need to re-learn how to interact with them, which will be easier for some than others. If you are more extroverted, maybe this will be easier for you. If you are an introvert, you may find this very challenging.

In any case, once again, you can't overcome social anxiety by sitting in your room watching TV shows, burying yourself in Social Media or playing video games. Using compensating behaviours like drinking alcohol and using drugs are also not helpful, for many reasons. You need to exercise your social intelligence and communication muscles in a concrete and lasting way and that means getting out there and interacting with people without props and crutches, which can be very daunting at first.

Again, one of the best ways to do this is to enter a shared frame of reference through a common activity like voluntary work, paid work or education. It is much more difficult to do where the frames of reference are vague such as meeting friends in a bar for example, or in more random situations where you don't know where people are coming from.

I want to emphasise again here that receiving counselling can be extremely helpful for overcoming social anxiety. When you have a therapeutic relationship with a counsellor, you are developing your communication and social skills in a safe space where you can freely express your worries and anxieties without the fear of being judged or excluded.

CBT techniques can also be extremely useful in social anxiety related situations. You can take some time to analyse what is going on for you in the moments that trigger your anxiety as you are probably stuck in a vicious negative thought cycle:

Action:
Identify your fear.

What is it that you think will happen that is so bad when you interact with this person or group?

Do your fears stop you from interacting in the first place? Do you make excuses such as 'I'm busy'? Are you afraid of embarrassing yourself?

What evidence do you have that your fear is justified? If your fear actually happens in reality, what is the very worst that could happen? Think it through, visualise it. Is it really so bad?

What negative 'self talk', beliefs, assumptions, sensations go on before, during and after you enter a social situation? Are you sabotaging yourself before you even start by being overly self-critical? Can you challenge your beliefs and assumptions? Are they based on anything? Can you try reversing them? 'I am amazing!', 'I am a social hero!', 'everybody likes and respects me', 'I don't need alcohol to have a good time'.

When you tested the interaction, was your fear justified, or were you pleasantly surprised?

What behaviours are you engaging in that may be sustaining this cycle? For example, not making eye contact, not speaking, not asking questions, focusing on negative sensations like blushing, sweating or shaking, drinking too much. Do you engage in negative post-morteming of the interaction - thinking 'I looked stupid' for example. Can you change any of these behaviours or focus on other things?

Communication Skills
There is a very interesting book that was written in the 1930's by Dale Carnegie called 'How to Win Friends and Influence People'. It was really aimed at business and marketing people,

but it was really well researched and contains some great advice about human communication. It can be useful to remember some of these points if you find communication challenging. Here are a few of them that I find particularly useful in day to day situations, mixed up with a few embellishments of my own:

Smile: A smile costs nothing and simply makes people feel good and at ease.

Use your voice and actually speak to people! Even if it is just a hello. Do it as much as possible. In shops, on the street, on public transport. Try to get used to just chatting to people with no particular outcome in mind. See it as a kind of workout / social muscle building exercise without having any attachment to a particular outcome.

'Remember that a person's name is to that person the sweetest and most important sound in any language': ...so ask them their name. This one is for when your conversation develops a little further than just superficial pleasantries and you don't already know the other person. If you do know the other person, remember their name and use it!

Become genuinely interested in other people: ...and talk in terms of the other person's interests.

Be a good listener: Encourage others to talk about themselves. Asking questions is one of the best ways to enter into conversation with people, and for most of us, the most interesting topic of any conversation is ourselves (even if we don't like to admit it!).

Make the other person feel important – and do it sincerely: Try to listen out for the things that you find genuinely interesting and that you appreciate about what the other person has to say. You may not feel like you agree with them or that you click with them completely but you can probably find at least some aspect that you can identify with and show interest in what they have to say.

'Give honest and sincere appreciation': (don't confuse this with praise, there is a difference) Expressing appreciation gives the other person a good feeling. Why wouldn't you want to give them that gift? But it must be genuine and sincere. If you are being fake, it is better to keep your mouth shut!

'Don't criticise, condemn or complain': I really like Carnegie's words on criticism. Criticism is one of the easiest things in the world to do and it is an easy, and dare I say it lazy habit to get into. The same goes for condemning and complaining.

> *Criticism is futile because it puts a person on the defensive and usually   makes him strive to justify himself. Criticism is dangerous, because it wounds a person's precious pride, hurts his sense of importance, and arouses resentment. ...Any fool can criticize, condemn and complain - and most fools do. But it takes character and self-control to be understanding and forgiving.*

> Dale Carnegie

Some people are natural communicators and find it very easy. For others, it is not so easy, but fortunately, it is a skill that we can develop and learn and there are many great tools out there to help. Of course, the first thing that you need to do is actually speak to people, which can seem terrifying if you have just come out of a psychotic episode. In this case, you can take some baby steps to get yourself into the swing of things like getting into the habit of making eye contact with random people, smiling at them, saying hello, asking them simple questions like 'how's your morning going?' etc. Once you get used to doing these things on a daily basis, it will become more and more natural to start conversations with people and to not feel like it is such a big deal to communicate with them.

One of the tricks here is not to be invested in any kind of outcome from your interactions. Be light hearted, even if you don't feel it at first, throw in some jokes or amusing comments. Not easy sometimes I know, especially if you have been in a deep dark hole, but don't overthink it. Just remember that the world, including people will tend to reflect back to you what you project into it. Some people will like to talk, others will not. You don't know what is going on for another person, what their story is, what their mood is that day, so don't worry if they don't respond to you in a way that you feel comfortable with. Just be respectful and move on. Other people may surprise you and make you laugh!

Once you have developed your 'communication muscles', it will start to feel much more natural for you to strike up conversations and interact with people in a confident and self assured way. This can make life a lot richer and lead us to having experiences and opportunities that we might not have imagined possible before.

THE BIGGER PICTURE

*Setting Some Long Term Goals
and Creating and Action Plan*

I n 5 years time, in an ideal world, how would you like your life to be? If you could order a new life on Amazon, what would it be? Brainstorm a list. Write down everything you can think of, don't leave anything out, don't hold back. Have confidence. How do you want to feel? How do you want to think? What do you want to be doing? What do you want to have achieved? What do you want to have? What are your heart's desires? Give yourself permission to do this exercise. It is useful. You have a future, you can create it.

Your list can be updated regularly because circumstances can change and so can your capacities. It is also really helpful to put your list in a place where you can see it regularly, and read it regularly to keep it in the front of your mind. If you have clearly defined goals, you will find that your subconscious mind has an uncanny ability to start to guide you towards the actions that you need to take in order to achieve them. By now, you know very well through your experience of psychosis how powerful your mind can be, so take advantage of that knowledge and make it work for you!

As well as writing a list of how you would like your life to be in

5 years time, it is also useful to write down a list of all the ways that you don't want your life to be in 5 years time. This really helps to increase our clarity and to separate things that we want from the things we don't want which helps us to make better choices on a day to day basis. What negative influences, thought patterns, self talk would you like to have transformed or eliminated? What negative habits would you like to have overcome? Write them all down and again, put your list next to your list of goals and read it regularly, updating it regularly also as your circumstances evolve and your capacities change.

Don't worry if you can't think of anything immediately to write on your lists. If you are very fresh out of a crisis, you may not be able to think much at all. In that case, just rest. It is enough to know that you can do this exercise in the future, you will remember that it exists, that it is useful and that you can come back to it later when you are ready.

Once you have made your list of goals, now is the time to make an action plan. What steps do you need to take in order to achieve your goals? What skills do you need to develop? What hoops will you need to jump through? What support can you obtain to help you to achieve your goals? Brainstorm a list of everything you can think of. Do some research into your areas of interest and find out what is required. Once you have a list of steps that you need to take, then try to prioritise it into high, medium and low priority tasks. Split it up into digestible chunks and then go for it!

Of course, what actually happens in five years time may be nothing like you imagined it. It depends on your goal. Circumstances change and it is impossible to predict the future. What is important is the journey itself, the participation, the sense of development and progression. Not necessarily the goal itself. The important thing is to choose a goal that you feel interested in, excited and passionate about.

It is beyond the scope of this book to go too far into this as what we are talking about here is basically life-coaching and there are a huge amount of great resources online to help you to move forward in this area. I really enjoyed and was motivated by reading the books and blog of Tim Ferriss for example and some of the work of Tony Robbins. You can check them out.

WORKING WITH
DEPRESSION AND
ANXIETY

I t is likely if you are recovering from psychosis, that depression and anxiety are familiar companions for you. I am afraid that I cannot offer any magical solution to help you to overcome these two states except to remember that they are exactly that, states. States can be changed, modified and manipulated and are impermanent so hang in there! The other advice that I can offer is really to apply the exact same methods that I have outlined in this book until now. You need to think in terms of depression and anxiety as being a result of disordered and uncoordinated Energy. So all of the methods that I have outlined are equally applicable for working with depression and anxiety as they are for helping you to recover from psychosis. There are a few additional points that I would like to highlight about working with depression and anxiety below.

Depression

Like all kinds of suffering, depression has its causes. Once you can identify the causes of your depression, it is much easier to find solutions, so it can be useful to do a little detective work to try to find out what the causes of your depression are. Again, it can be really useful to work with a counsellor, CBT or psychotherapist who will have an objective view of your situation in order to identify these causes. If your depression is severe, you should consult with your doctor and use antidepressant medication if necessary. The cause of your depression may by physiological. At the same time, you can use the advice in this guide to help to build internal tools and resources to help you to overcome or manage your condition more effectively going forward.

As a Chinese medicine practitioner, I find that some of the imagery used in Chinese medicine can be a useful starting point for understanding some of the mechanisms of depression. In Chinese Medicine, depression is very often connected with the 'Liver'. The Liver in Chinese medicine is responsible for the smooth flow of Energy around the body and the element associated with the Liver is Wood. The nature of the Wood element is expansion, upwards and outwards, downwards and inwards.

When in balance, nutrients and Energy are conducted smoothly through the vessels of the body. Much like a tree will conduct and distribute nutrients from the earth through the roots to every branch and leaf. On a mental and emotional level, the mood is good and the Mind is agile, flexible, fluid, light and clear and decisions are made with confidence.

When this expansion and distribution is constrained, either physically through illness, poor diet or lack of exercise, or mentally, through desires or emotions being thwarted or blocked by external circumstances or internal limitations, pressure can build, leading to consequences for our mental and physical health. Constraint leads to stagnation of our Energy system which makes us feel lethargic and tired. Our mood becomes low and jaded and our Mind loses it's agile, flexible, fluid, clear quality and it becomes much more difficult to confidently make decisions.

Because there is Energy there that has been constrained and blocked, the pressure of it grows because it cannot move. If the pressure grows sufficiently, then frustration, anxiety, anger and even rage can be generated. This is much like when a tree grows through concrete or stone with roots that have become twisted and gnarled by virtue of the huge energy, pressure and constraint that accumulated, eventually leading the concrete or stone to crack and break. This kind of constraint and stagnation can be hugely destructive.

Constraint and stagnation can also be reflected in the unpleasant physical manifestations that are often associated with depression such as digestive problems, aches and pains, malaise, headaches, and according to Chinese medicine, even masses and tumors, much like the hard knots we see developing in trees.

Action:

Using the Chinese medicine approach, a good way of working with depression can be to look at the ways in which you are restricted or constrained. Constraint can take many forms both external and internal. Make some lists or flow charts of the things that constrain you both internally and externally and think of ways in which you can address them.

For example, internal constraint could take the form of not expressing your desires in an effective way, like when you are in a relationship and your partner keeps doing something that really annoys you but you don't say anything. Rather than honouring yourself and your desires and needs, you block them in order to 'please' your partner. This leads to constraint and eventual resentment on your part, because you are not expressing your needs, and resentment on the part of your partner, because you are essentially being dishonest with them, and they can sense it. It would be much better to freely express your feelings in a respectful way.

Internal constraint could also take the form of negative self talk. For example, telling yourself that you are not good enough at something, like making new friends for example. The more you tell yourself that is the case, the more true it becomes. You start to put less and less effort into it, and as a result, become less and less good at it. Then you feel isolated, lonely, frustrated, blocked, possibly ashamed and later depressed. If you reversed that self talk cycle, you could free up that blocked Energy and channel it into working at improving your befriending skills, leading to becoming better and better communicator and giver. Then instead of feeling frustrated and blocked, you will feel the opposite of stagnation, a wholesome feeling of the satisfaction of progression and the fulfilment of your desire to make friends.

With external obstacles and constraints, what becomes important is how you deal with the situation. For example, if you apply for a job and are rejected, a positive, unconstrained way to deal with this would be to embrace the feelings of frustration and disappointment and allow them to flow through you and perhaps to drive you into the action (movement) of contacting the prospective employer and asking them for feedback on your application so that you can take steps to improve your employment game and make an action plan. A negative, constrained (stagnant) way to deal with this would be to become downhearted and resentful, entering into a passive mode and falling into negative self talk about how you are not good enough, that there is too much competition, that you are unemployable. This second response would be a pathway to an inactive and depressive mindset.

Another important way to combat depression is to generate a sense of purpose and progression towards goals. A common feature of depression can be a feeling that there are so many choices, but that they are all pointless. Why choose one thing over another when everything is meaningless? One then becomes totally passive and stagnant. It requires a bit of effort to lift oneself out of this mindset and a good way to do this is to practice setting goals and achieving them as mentioned above, starting small and then expanding as your confidence, inspiration and motivation increase.

Anxiety

I have always had a tendency towards feeling anxious, but a while back I was confronted by my anxiety head on and couldn't brush it aside and ignore it any more. I was driving down the motorway and started to feel this sense that the world was closing in on me, a deep panic started to rise up from my feet towards my chest. I started to feel that I couldn't get a full breath. I felt hot and clammy and worried that I was going to pass out or even die. I had passengers in the car at the time so on top of the feelings of panic, I had a strong feeling of fear that I may harm them along with shame and inadequacy. There was an internal conflict of feeling the panic but at the same time, trying to 'keep it together', to both keep the car on the road and not to injure anyone and also the perceived 'social' pressure to not show weakness or vulnerability. Eventually, I couldn't handle it anymore, pulled over, and asked someone else to drive. My friends were very understanding and didn't judge me at all and it was both humbling and liberating to admit that I wasn't coping at that point. After that experience, it was very difficult for me to drive on the motorway for quite some time, but it made me have to start to find ways of dealing with my anxiety more effectively.

Again, it is really useful if you have the possibility to work with a counsellor, CBT or psychotherapist in order to get to the bottom of your anxiety issues. Through my own exploration of anxiety, I discovered that it was largely the result of unacknowledged, repressed, buried emotions that had accumulated over a long period of time. The only way to overcome my anxiety was to dive deep into these emotions and experience and feel them fully. This meant putting some real effort into really connecting with myself in a very deep way.

We repress, ignore and bury difficult emotions for many different reasons. Because we are traumatised, because we do not have the maturity or skills to be able to process them effectively, because we are under pressure and don't have the time or energy to deal with them or because we don't want to feel uncomfortable things. It may also be that we have been taught to 'keep our chins up' and plough on, that looking at difficult emotions is self indulgent and weak.

What happens though is that when we repress these emotions, they become displaced in our psyche, like orphaned abandoned children. They get stuck where they are and are not integrated and cannot move on. In psychosis, they even start to appear to us as something outside of ourselves such as voices and persecutory delusions. When we suffer from anxiety, we are subconsciously hearing the cries of these displaced and abandoned children and they are agitating our Minds and disordering our Energy. Ignorance is not bliss in this case, it is a timebomb, a disaster waiting to happen. When at its peak, these abandoned children will group together and form a rebellious army that attacks, demanding to be heard and resulting panic for their host and keeping us awake at night with insomnia.

In order to heal our anxiety, we really need to become a kind, loving mother to ourselves. Noone else will do this for us. We need to open our arms to our neglected emotion-children, greet them, embrace them, accept them without judgement, love them, give them time and attention, be with them through thick and thin, feel their sensations and emotions fully to the point where they relax, mature and are reintegrated.

Action:
If you feel anxious, first, if possible, eliminate any obvious external causes that may be present that you can do something about. For example, paying outstanding bills, filling in your tax return, apologising to a friend if you did something to upset them. This is like clearing the deck of a boat, or tidying up your room.

Then, especially when your anxiety becomes really overwhelming you need to take some time out. Go to a quiet place. Go to your room and close the curtains. Lie down.

Now you need to enter the role of the loving mother who is befriending her long lost, traumatised child. You need to connect with your feelings, with your body, with your sensations and the way to do this is by using your breath. Your breath is the mother of your life. Don't get involved with your mental concepts or thought cascades around the feelings, you need to adopt a spacious quality, use your breath to do this, to give space to your feelings, to allow them to breathe, breathe into them deeply and profoundly.

Very often, the anxiety that you feel will be connected with a physical sensation, often in your chest or abdomen, but it could be anywhere. You need to breathe into that sensation and notice when you feel tension in your body. Breathe into the tension and relax it. Feel the sensation fully, acknowledge it, breathe into it, give it space and relax as much as you can. As you go deeper, you will start to feel the emotions more fully. There could be fear, worry, doubt, confusion, trauma, terror, anything that arises. Use your breath, greet your emotions, embrace them with your in and out breaths, be loving towards them like a mother would be, give them time and acceptance, don't judge them, don't flinch away from them.

Remember your body. When you notice how the emotion or feeling makes you tense up, move around a bit and try to relax. Then go back into it again with your breathing. It is very important to alternate relaxation with breathing into your emotions. Relaxation of tension here is the goal.

At times, you may feel overwhelmed. This is ok. If it is too much, then just stop. Relax, move around, go for a walk, do something else. You can always come back to it again. Cry if you need to without holding back. Crying is good. It is movement, it is a release, it is a liberation of your blocked Energy.

When you become more familiar with this process, it becomes much easier and you can go deeper quicker and become more resilient and accepting when confronted with truly unpleasant feelings and sensations that have been accumulated over the years.

After a while the tension begins to subside and the emotions will relax and start to reintegrate into you. The dualism of 'this is me' and 'this is my emotion or feeling' will diminish. Your abandoned traumatised children start to find their confidence, to grow up, relax and move towards your embrace. These feelings and emotions are in some way like globules of tension in our psyche. Once they relax, they can reintegrate. When this happens, you may feel a warm, nourishing, glowing feeling throughout your body combined with a deeper sense of stability and confidence. You will feel more complete.

RELATIONSHIPS & INTIMACY

You may wonder why I am including a section on relationships and intimacy in a recovery guide for psychosis. The reason is that the capacity to have healthy, intimate relationships, or at least to know and be comfortable with oneself in this area, is an important part of the completeness and richness of our human experience.

Through the experience of psychosis, we may have completely lost our confidence and self esteem, even if prior to the experience, we were full of those things. This can limit our ability to connect with others due to fear and anxiety and also lead us to connect with others in unhealthy ways out of insecurity. It is also possible that we may have lost interest in the things that we used to enjoy, including people and become withdrawn.

If we had difficulties in our families in early childhood, relationships can also strongly trigger these vulnerabilities which may well have come to the surface as a result of psychosis. For these reasons, I think it is important to explore this area a little and provide a small map for further exploration should you want or need to go deeper. In this section of the guide, I will share some of the things that I have picked up on my own journey of discovery that may be helpful for you.

As I said earlier, this guide is something that I am putting together with the beautiful assistance of hindsight. It was actually through my exploration into relationship issues after a difficult breakup a few years back which put me in a pretty wobbly state for a while, that I embarked on the road of counselling and psychotherapy. I came to understand the value of therapy and how it can be useful for psychosis recovery through exploring current relationship issues and then going deeper into my past and delving into the causes of my psychosis. I also became aware that my habit would be to avoid intimacy because it would trigger the seething mass of insecurity that I had bubbling away in my psyche which in turn triggered my fear of losing my hard won mental stability.

Fortunately, like communication skills, and very much related to communication skills, this is an area that we can learn to develop if we want to. There are skills that we can learn to help us to work-out our relationship and intimacy muscles. Again, I am in no way an expert in this area and I am still developing and learning, and probably always will be, but I have found a few things that have been useful for me on my journey so far, and my relationship experiences are becoming more and more positive and healthy as a result. Maybe they will be useful for you too.

One of the key things that I have come to understand is about attachment to outcomes, if we have an open and relaxed attitude, everything goes better. If we become very attached to our need and desire to obtain something from someone else (love, attention, validation, sex, security), then everything becomes more problematic. It is best to feel complete and whole in oneself and not look for someone else to complete us. That way, our intimate relationships will have a lighter, more joyful touch.

If you are entering a relationship out of need and insecurity (which is what I always did), then there is already a problem. It is better to get on top of that and meet your own needs and address your insecurities to the extent to which you feel pretty good about yourself, your occupation, your friends and your place in the world. If you feel insecure, it is good to at least recognise this and take some time to understand what triggers your insecurities and do something to address those things. If you can manage that, then your relationship will be less loaded with expectations (that are unlikely to be met) and dependencies (that lead to imbalances which cause tension) and is likely to be far more fulfilling for both partners. Not to mention that expectations and dependencies based on need are total attraction killers.

Of course there are no perfect relationships, they all require care and attention and they will all have their ups and downs. There is no perfect time to start a relationship and we always need to work with our circumstances, but it is helpful to understand and take an active interest in relationships and our own relationship with relationships. Many of us wander blindly in this area without really taking the time to 'get on top of the horse' and understand ourselves. We need to learn as much as we can in order to do our best to develop our relationships in as healthy a way as possible.

Understanding Security &
Insecurity in Relationships

You have probably noticed that there are some people who find relationships and intimacy to be fairly effortless in terms of meeting people, becoming intimate with them and forming long term relationships. When they have breakups, they tend to move on fairly quickly to their next long term relationship. There are others who find it difficult to meet people and become intimate with them, and even if they do, it is hard for them to maintain a stable relationship for any length of time. I was really intrigued by this and looked into it because I personally found it very hard to make lasting intimate connections even before I suffered from psychosis and then much harder afterwards until I managed to get myself a bit more together.

When I discovered adult attachment theory, through a book by Amir Levine and Rachel Heller (see the Resources section below), I was kicking myself that I hadn't had the chance to learn about it as a teenager because it would have helped me a lot to understand what was going on. It's the kind of thing that I think they should teach in schools! Later, after having started to go through psychotherapy, I discovered that the model is quite simplistic, but at least as a starting point, it provides a useful frame of reference in order to make some sense of this often confusing area of life, particularly if you are an insecure attachment type (that's 50% of the population. You are not alone!).

In a nutshell, Adult Attachment Theory goes something like this:

Research shows that during childhood, more or less 50% of people will develop a secure attachment relationship with their primary caregiver (from now on referred to as their mother, but it could be the father or guardian depending on the situation). 50% will develop an insecure attachment relationship.

These early attachment styles have a huge impact on the kinds of relationships those children will have in the future as adults.

It is most desirable to be a secure attachment type. Insecure attachment types are much more likely to have problems with their relationships.

There are three types of insecure attachment, Anxious, Avoidant (evasive) and Disordered. More or less 35% of insecure attachment types are Anxious and the other 35% are Avoidant. The remaining percentage of insecure types will swing between Anxious and Avoidant and this pattern is referred to as Disordered.

Disordered Insecure Attachment in particular has been associated with Psychosis and Schizophrenia and is often the result of abuse, inconsistent availability and attentiveness to the needs of the child from the primary caregiver.

Secure Attachment

Fortunate people with secure attachment will have received consistently attentive responses to their physical and emotional needs during the most impressionable parts of their childhood from their mother, that will have cemented their sense of security, self worth and autonomy. They feel confident in their expression of vulnerability and their reception of love and affection and are more confident in exploring their environment because they are secure in the knowledge that their caregiver has their back and will be there for them no matter what.

These are the people who tend to find relationships fairly easy going and they are confident that they will find the emotional support that they need. They tend to have stable, long term, relatively undramatic relationships, are good communicators and have fewer problems expressing love, affection and intimacy.

Anxious Insecure Attachment

The causes of any given attachment style are complex, and people with anxious insecure attachment among other things are likely to have received inconsistent attentiveness and responsiveness to their needs from their mother as a child. Sometimes they will have been there for them, but other times not. This generates a complex set of emotions in the child where there is anxiety that their mother is not present for them along with a strong longing and need for their attention and love. However, this longing can be combined with huge anger and resentment towards their mother for not being available for them when they were needed. When their mother does finally become available for them, the anxiously attached child will often push them away and display angry, resentful behaviour towards them. Anxious, insecurely attached children do not feel so confident when exploring their environment and will tend to be fearful, timid and untrusting that their partners will be really available for them.

These are the people who have problems in relationships because they tend to be needy and do not feel like they are good enough or deserve to be loved. They tend to put a huge emphasis on their relationships and obsess over them because of their underlying insecurity that it will be 'taken away' and they are not good enough. Of course they often end up unintentionally pushing other people away because of their insecurity, which then reinforces their view that they are not good enough.

A secure attachment type in comparison is unlikely to go through any of these insecure thought processes at all, or if they do, they will not pay much importance to them.

Avoidant Insecure Attachment

Avoidant insecure types will have often had caregivers that are emotionally unavailable, out of tune and consistently unresponsive to or dismissive of their needs. In this case, the child tends to avoid situations in which they will be exposed to an emotional need in order to avoid being rebuffed by the emotionally unavailable caregiver. They essentially feel like they are wrong if they have some kind of emotional need and feel shame if they have to express one.

Avoidant attachment types are those that tend to push people away and not let them get close to them. The problem is that deep down, they are doing this out of insecurity. While they may give the impression of being strong, secure and independent, they actually crave love and support but associate this with being dismissed or unvalidated so avoid it because it makes them feel insecure. They are therefore wary of getting too close to other people.

In contrast, a secure attachment type would have very little difficulty in expressing their emotions, needs and desires and if they do feel uncomfortable or insecure about this, they do not pay too much importance to it because they have the underlying confidence that everything will be ok, and if it is not ok in the moment, whatever happens, they will be fine in the end.

The "Anxious-Avoidant Trap"

This is an example of how we can tend to choose relationships that are damaging for us because they are what we know, and because these damaging patterns were laid down within us at such an early age, that we rarely have adequate tools with which to question what is going on. We don't question these patterns because they are part of the fabric of who we are.

The "anxious-avoidant trap" is the most common type of relationship that is held between insecure attachment types. This kind of relationship has an addictive and dramatic quality to it where both partners will have their world views reinforced. The anxious person will be constantly preoccupied by the relationship, by the small things that the other person might have said and what it means for their relationship. Deep down the anxious person is sure that they are not good enough and they don't deserve to be loved, even though that is what they desperately want. The avoidant person very much wants to be loved and adored too and at the beginning of the relationship will find the lavish attention that they receive from the anxious partner to be exciting and passionate. There can be huge passionate fireworks for the anxious-avoidant couple.

Then, what happens is that the avoidant partner will find themselves withdrawing from their anxious partner because they are finding the attention cloying and it is inhibiting their need for freedom and is triggering their insecurity that the love that they receive will be laden with rules and conditions or that the love that they give will be dismissed if they open up. This withdrawal will trigger the anxious partner's concerns, which leads to needy behaviour, which in turn leads the avoidant partner to withdraw even more and the cycle continues. Eventually the avoidant partner will most likely leave the relationship and the anxious partner is likely to come off worse because of their high level of investment in the relationship.

As time passes, the avoidant partner will start to miss the attention that they used to receive and begin to crave it and move on to someone else while at the same time, often idealising the previous relationship and mooning over it. At this point, when they meet someone new, they may display the 'phantom-ex' behaviour where they are always comparing their current partner to their previous one, which is of course is a way of sabotaging the relationship from the start and not getting too close. If they end up getting back together with their ex, there will be passionate sexual fireworks and euphoria but it will be short lived once the cycle starts again and the anxious partners neediness resurfaces.

The most healthy thing for all insecure attachment types is to find a partner who is secure and to learn how to become secure oneself. It has been observed that it is possible that the security of the secure type tends to 'rub off' on their insecure partners and their insecurities tend to subside over time. The problem here is that in general, secure attachment types tend to enter into long term committed relationships quite early on in their lives, so they do not tend to show up in the dating pool. For this reason, it is worth being aware of the possibility that the majority of people in the dating pool will be insecure attachment types.

There can be a couple of issues that come up for insecure attachment types when entering into a relationship with a secure attachment type. The first being that the lack of drama associated with a relationship with a secure person makes the insecurely attached partners feel like they are not 'in love', that there is 'no passion', that it is boring. The anxious-avoidant relationship is a roller coaster of passion and drama which is addictive and these attachment types associate this drama with being 'in love'. Secure relationships are more slow burning with a perhaps deeper and more supportive kind of love. Insecure attachment types are encouraged to be patient and give secure relationships a chance to grow because the long term rewards can be great.

Attachment Theory Takeaway

Okay so the main takeaways from attachment theory are these:

Being an insecure attachment type is not ideal.

Relationships between insecure attachment types are problematic and should be avoided if possible.

If you are an insecure attachment type, when choosing a partner, it is best to a) find someone who is a secure attachment type or b) learn how to become a secure attachment type yourself (by using therapy and by doing a lot of work on yourself). At the very least, be aware of your insecurity.

If you are an insecure attachment type, it is possible particularly through psychotherapy and working hard on yourself to learn how to become a secure attachment type.

Secure attachment types have been observed to have a healing effect on insecure partners over time, particularly anxious types, as the insecurely attached partner gradually realises that their worries are unfounded and they are able to grow their trust and to relax.

Relationship Compatibilities Between Attachment Types:

Anxious-Anxious: Unlikely to work unless their anxieties are 'complementary', but even in this case, it is unlikely to be smooth sailing.

Anxious-Avoidant: Dramatic roller coaster ride. The avoidant type is most likely to come out on top in this kind of relationship as they will be the one to withdraw and will invest less, while the anxious person is likely to become more and more anxious.

Avoidant-Avoidant: Unlikely to last more than a few days or weeks. There is not much to connect two avoidant people.

Secure-Insecure: Good for all insecure types if they can be patient and give it time. Secure partners need to be aware that their security can be undermined by a particularly insecure partner and that they can be drawn into an insecure state themselves. Treasure your security. It is a great gift.

Secure-Secure: Healthy, stable, secure, supportive, easy communication.

If you are in any of the above relationship patterns in your existing relationship, understanding the principles of attachment theory may help you to understand your relationship much more deeply and some of the issues that may arise. If you are not in a relationship, this information may help you to understand some of the patterns that you tend to follow around relationships in order to help you make better informed choices in the future.

Of course, this is a very much simplified exploration of attachment theory and there are many great resources that can be found about this online and through authors such as Amir Levine and Rachel Heller.

FOOD & DRINK
HABITS THAT HELP
CALM THE MIND

When I went to University, I chose to study Traditional Chinese Medicine, mostly because I wanted to understand more about my own condition and then hopefully to be able to do some kind of work afterwards that was beneficial to people. I also learned some things about Tibetan medicine through studying the work of my teacher Namkhai Norbu Rinpoche. The main principle is to understand that everything is interdependent, particularly in relation to our health and a huge factor that affects the quality of our health is the way we eat.

> *Eating is like sowing a field with grain.*
> *Likewise, with a healthy diet, one's digestive*
> *warmth is maintained, and this leads to a "har-*
> *vest" of good health. An unhealthy diet, on the*
> *other hand, impairs one's digestive warmth,*
> *which then damages one's health.*

> Dr Yeshi Dhonden

We all know that there are certain foods and combinations of foods that stimulate us, like sugar and caffeine, and others that make us dull and sleepy, like pasta and meat. Tibetan medicine in particular offers some good advice on what foods to consume and what foods to avoid in order to reduce problems with *Lung* or subtle Wind that I mentioned before which can make us feel nervous or agitated.

Now I personally had a huge resistance to doing much with my own diet until quite recently, mostly because I am a carbohydrate / sugar addict and I was resistant to making any changes. Since making a concerted effort to drop added sugar from my diet and to reduce my carbohydrate intake, I have a bit more clarity about diet and a bit more capacity not to be dominated by my previous habits. But I don't want to get too complicated about diet here because it is a minefield that can lead to an extra layer of stress, so I will give a few indicators of general principles so as to try to keep it simple.

Food First Aid

He who takes medicine and neglects the diet,
wastes the skill of his doctors.

Chinese Proverb

If you are feeling anxious, agitated or are having problems sleeping. It means that your Energy is disordered and needs to be calmed down. Here are a few simple dietary principles that you can try to adopt that may help. They are also good general principles to adopt anyway, whether you have a disordered Energy system or not:

Eat Regularly at the Same Times Each Day: As I mentioned before, the body loves rhythm and this very much includes dietary rhythm. It reduces a certain amount of ambient stress for our bodies if we eat at regular times. Try not to skip meals either. You need to be well nourished.

Don't Overeat: In Chinese medicine, it is recommended that we never eat until we are 100% full in order not to 'overload' our digestive system and make it weak. This can create problems with stagnation, phlegm and damp. Rather, it is recommended that we eat until we are 70% full, always leaving a little hunger at the end of each meal. We should always leave our bodies wanting just a little bit more at the end of each meal rather than stuffing ourselves until we are full.

Don't Undereat: Undereating is also not good. It makes us tired, creates a low mood and creates a kind of 'vacuum' in our blood which generates problems with internal Wind (Lung) and makes us nervous and anxious and causes problems with sleep.

In Chinese Medicine, the Shen or 'consciousness' is considered to be housed in the blood while we sleep. It is like a warm, comfortable, nourishing nest in which the consciousness can reside. If the blood is not nourished well, instead of it being a warm, comfortable, nourishing place for the consciousness to rest, it can become a stark, uninviting environment that leads the consciousness to find somewhere else to go which results in restlessness and insomnia.

Eat Slow Cooked Soups with Bones (or equivalent): Slow cooked soups made with boiled bones and with red meat like beef or mutton are some of the best foods for this kind of problem. You can also use chicken. Cook yourself up a big pot of it and eat it every day throughout the week, particularly in the evenings. You can include copious amounts of any kinds of vegetables you like, especially green vegetables and it is fine to add some potatoes, barley or rice etc but don't go overboard. It can be good to add herbs like fresh ginger, Goji berries, dates, nutmeg and turmeric (curcuma). If you are a vegetarian, you'll need to leave out the bones and meat, but especially include lots of green vegetables and lots of deep, dark beans such as black beans or kidney beans.

When doing this, use a good amount of <u>butter</u> or oils like olive oil or sesame oil.

If in Doubt, Eat Simple, Bland Foods: If you are not sure what foods to eat that would be best for your health, or you don't have any energy or motivation to think too much about your diet, then as well as the soups mentioned above, eat simple bland foods that are neutral in flavour and that are not cooked too heavily in oils and fats. A perfect example of this would be steamed fish with some steamed rice and lots of steamed green vegetables with some butter. Apart from soups with vegetables and bones, this is pretty much the perfect type of food that it is difficult to go wrong with. You can flavour it with a little salt or soy sauce, but keep it really simple, remembering to only eat until you are 70% full. It is also very easy to prepare this kind of food so it is really a no brainer.

Aged Red Wine: Drink a quarter or half glass of aged red wine with your lunch and dinner, or a tablespoon of rum, brandy or whisky (unless you are taking a medication that prohibits alcohol intake or have a problem with alcohol addiction).

Nevereat or drink cold or raw foods: If you dump a whole bunch of iced drinks or cold foods into your stomach, your stomach has to work twice as hard to first warm the food up and then get down to the business of digesting it and transforming it into nourishment for your blood and energy. This kind of habit damages the digestive warmth of the stomach, making it weak over time which can lead to problems such as indigestion, bloating and nausea. The same principle goes for raw foods. When food is raw, the stomach has to work twice as hard to digest and transform it which is depleting. At the very least, the food or drink that you consume should be at room temperature, but ideally should be warm or hot.

In Tibetan medicine, the quality of the *Lung* (Wind) energy that makes us agitated is cold so generally we want to avoid anything that is cold in nature unless we have a very hot constitution.

Don't Eat Products with Added Sugar & Quit Adding Sugar

Yourself: I already talked about this in the section above on insomnia. If we have stable blood sugar levels, our Energy becomes more smooth and stable and therefore we can be more relaxed, calm and clear. Refined sugar is extremely addictive while at the same time being totally useless in terms of our actual nutrition. It is like the Facebook newsfeed of foods, it is attractive enough for you to 'click' onto and buy and gives a certain lift when you eat it but ultimately leaves you feeling empty and dissatisfied, just wanting more.

Drink Warm or Hot Fluids After Meals: After meals, in order to aid your digestive heat and the digestive processes, it is really good to get into the habit of drinking hot water or some kind of tea such as fennel tea or fresh ginger tea.

COMPLEMENTARY THERAPIES

The world of complementary therapies can be quite bewildering as there are so many of them and it is hard to know which, if any of them will help you. At the same time, in order to find out, you can be spending anything from £25 - £125 a time and you will need at least three sessions with your therapist in order to find out if it is helping you. That said, if a therapy helps you to feel relaxed and helps to coordinate your Body, Energy and Mind then it is valuable. The key thing is to remember that these treatments are complementary and that they should not be a replacement for medical treatment with your doctor.

There has been quite a lot of research that has been conducted with GP's that show that they feel that a very large percentage of the therapeutic value of their work is not so much in the treatments that they offer but the attention and the reassurance that they give their patients. One of the wonderful things about many types of complementary therapies is that they provide a space in which you can receive dedicated support and attention from another human being for at least 30 minutes to 1 hour each time. Because suffering from psychosis or any kind of mental health issue can be very isolating, it can be very life affirming and nourishing to receive any kind of complementary therapy, for the dedicated contact and attention that is devoted to you alone, quite apart from any therapeutic value of the particular treatment that they are offering. It is a humanising experience.

If the therapy that you choose involves touch, like massage for example, this can also be very good because the isolation that goes along with mental health problems can also mean that we do not actually have any physical human contact. If we receive some physical contact through a therapy, this can help us to feel embodied and validated, that we do in fact exist. It also helps us to relax, which is important.

Low Cost Solutions

I am adding this note to the beginning of this section to offer a little inspiration to you if you are short on funds. If you are recovering from psychosis, it is likely that you will not be working and that your income will be restricted, unless you have a good sick pay package from your employer, good health insurance or ample savings. If you are low on funds then there are a few things that you can try in order to negotiate low cost treatments for the therapy that you choose.

Student Clinics: Most therapy schools have special low cost clinics that are used in order to train their students. Try doing a search for therapy schools in your area (including adult education colleges) for a particular therapy that you are interested in and see if they run a low cost clinic.

Negotiate Discounted Rates: Many therapists will try to help people on low incomes if they can and may have allocated a certain amount of low cost slots per week for their clients in their schedules. It is a case of if you don't ask, you don't know!

Another thing you can try is to commit to going regularly if they offer you a discounted rate. My experience as a therapist is that it is much better for me that someone comes for ten sessions at £30 per session than one or two sessions at £60 for example.

Offer a Skill Swop: If you can't afford even the discounted rates (which can also seem daunting at times), maybe there is a skill that you have that you can offer to the therapist in exchange for treatments. Is there something that you can offer in exchange, like gardening? Helping them with advertising? (most therapists are not natural marketers in my experience), cleaning their car? Have a think and ask, but be careful to respect the boundaries of the therapist and don't push them.

Recommended Therapies

There are such a huge variety of complementary therapies out there, many of which I am pretty sceptical about. I think an attitude of healthy scepticism is important in this area because some people tend to make some pretty outlandish claims that can prey on the hopes and fears of vulnerable people.

As with counselling and psychotherapy, the best thing to do is to get recommendations for good therapists from trusted friends. If you have no recommendations, whatever therapist you choose, make sure that they are a member of a professional association for their particular therapy. This will give you confidence that they have undergone the correct training and a sufficient number of supervised clinical hours.

Acupuncture and Chinese Medicine: I trained in acupuncture and Chinese medicine, so of course I have many years of experience with that and have confidence in them as effective therapies both as a practitioner and as a patient.

The great thing about Chinese medicine is that the diagnostic system is advanced and the treatment principles and methods can go deep into the roots of problems. There is a profound understanding in Chinese medicine of how imbalances in the Energy level can affect the Mind level and vice versa and acupuncture can be very effective in addressing this, which is great for psychosis recovery while you are getting back on your feet. Chinese Herbal medicine formulas can also be very helpful to regulate your system but requires time and consistency. It is a waste of time and money if you do not commit to doing it consistently.

If you are feeling very anxious, sensitive or vulnerable, you may find it difficult to accept acupuncture treatment. Acupuncture is generally not an uncomfortable experience but if you are anxious about it and tense, it can become uncomfortable because your muscles tighten up in anticipation of the needles being inserted. In this case it may be better to ask your therapist for acupressure (Tunina) massage therapy instead until you feel more comfortable with the idea of acupuncture. You could also try Shiatsu which is based on Chinese medicine theory.

The quality of Chinese medicine treatments can vary a lot depending on the practitioner, so if possible try to get a recommendation from someone that you trust. Otherwise, you can find a therapist using the professional association websites. In the UK, these are the British Acupuncture Council (BAcC) for acupuncture and the Register of Chinese Herbal Medicine (RCHM) for Chinese herbal medicine. With regard to acupuncture, I particularly recommend seeking practitioners who have been trained in Japanese styles by teachers like Kiiko Matsumoto.

Shiatsu Massage: Shiatsu is a form of massage that developed from Chinese medicine as it entered Japan. It uses some of the same diagnostic methods and the same system of channels and pressure points with their corresponding therapeutic qualities. For this reason, it is an excellent therapy to choose if you are not comfortable with receiving acupuncture treatments.

Tibetan Medicine: Tibetan medicine is not very well known or easily accessible but has a fantastic diagnostic system which pays special attention to the *Lung* (Wind) disorders that I mentioned before which are particularly important for the treatment of mental health problems. The treatments of Tibetan medicine are mostly herb based, but the area where it is most useful for people in the West in my opinion is in its diet and lifestyle advice.

Do a search online and see if there is a Tibetan medicine practitioner in your area. I am not sure if there are any professional associations for Tibetan medicine so you will need to do a little detective work to find out if any practitioner that you find is in fact authentic.

Kunye Massage: Kunye massage is a Tibetan external therapy system that is based on the principles of Tibetan medicine using the same system of channels and pressure points. It is excellent for treating *Lung* (Wind) disorders that cause anxiety, nervousness and insomnia and includes the use of medicinal oils than are selected based on the needs of the patient.

Craniosacral Therapy: For me, craniosacral therapy is one of the most relaxing and profound manual therapies available. It is very subtle and simply involves the practitioner placing their hands under different parts of the head, neck, spine and sacrum. It is quite intuitive on the part of the practitioner and they will make small adjustments to the way they support your spine throughout the treatment. All you will need to do is relax and let go.

When I receive craniosacral therapy, it is one of the few things that I feel helps me to address some of those early childhood causes of insecurity, to relax and nourish that part of my psyche. Of course, your experience will depend quite a lot on how receptive you are and your connection with the practitioner and how you feel with them.

Massage Therapy: There are many types of massage therapy such as Holistic Massage, Sports Massage, Thai Massage. In my opinion, if you find a massage practitioner that you feel comfortable with, whatever the system, it is good. It is good to allow yourself to receive the attention of another, which can help to increase your confidence and help to reduce feelings of isolation that you may have. It is also really valuable to experience the power of physical touch.

Massage stimulates and helps to harmonise your Body by promoting circulation, it encourages you to relax your Energy by naturally breathing in more relaxed and deep way, and as a result of relaxed Body and Energy, also because you get to put yourself in the hands of another for a period of time, your Mind gets to relax too.

COMING OFF YOUR MEDICATION

As you start to feel better, you may reach a point where you sense that your medication is hindering you rather than helping you, because of the numbing effect it can have on your clarity and emotions. At some point, you will probably begin to think that you no longer wish to be dependent on medication in this way.

There is a lot of stigma around taking medication in order to maintain mental health, not to mention that it can be bruising for our sense of pride that we should need to be dependent on that. In any case, it is important not to take any reduction or withdrawal from medication lightly and you should always consult and collaborate with your doctor over this. It definitely should not be a casual, emotional decision. It is really important for you to be very aware that any sudden withdrawal from your medication can lead you straight back into a psychotic state. This also applies to withdrawal from antidepressants and anti-anxiety drugs.

> *...it is important not to take any reduction or withdrawal from medication lightly and you should always consult and collaborate with your doctor over this*

It is vital that if you are aiming to come off your medication that you do it very gradually. That means for example, if you are taking one tablet twice per day, you reduce each by 1/4 of a tablet for several weeks or even months until you feel ok with it. Then you reduce by another 1/4 for several weeks or months, and again for the following few weeks or months. This process could even take a year to two. There is no rush. The important thing is that it is managed safely in collaboration with your doctor. If you feel unstable or wobbly at any point, there is no shame in increasing the dose again to a level that you feel comfortable with until you feel like you have the capacity to give it another shot.

The principle here is to build up your tools, your foundations, your new frame of reference to such an extent that when you take the scaffolding away (medication in this case) piece by piece, that the house still stands up. As a starting point, you can develop your inner 'scaffolding' capacity by applying the methods and tools that I have outlined in this guide.

MOVING ON

I would like to remind you on the road to recovery, to always remember to be kind to yourself. Remember to judge your recovery by comparing yourself to yourself. Compare where you are today to where you were last week, or last month or last year. Be careful of comparing yourself to others. Having a mental illness is not like breaking a leg, where you and everyone around you know that your leg is broken, that you have to rest, and that after a period of time, it heals and you go back to life as normal. It is more complicated than that. It is not so easy for you or others to see your own recovery. It is not always obvious, and the path to recovery is not uniform and direct. It is complicated and convoluted.

When you experience setbacks, try to remember to zoom out and look at the big picture. Get some perspective. Look at how far you have come and really appreciate it and love yourself for it. If you need to talk to someone or ask for help, it is okay too.

THANK YOU!

W riting this guide has been a profound process for me. It has challenged me to shine a light on and to confront many aspects of myself and my history with psychosis and also ongoing issues such as insecurity, anxiety and depression. It has been a very nourishing and healing experience and feels like a closure of one cycle in my life while opening up a whole set of new horizons. I would like to thank you, from the bottom of my heart, for giving me the opportunity to go through this process so that I can offer it to you!

I really hope that by using this guide, you have found that you are able to gradually apply these tools and to feel similarly nourished and healed in your own way. Of course, one read-through will not be enough. You will need to keep coming back to it again and again in order to remind yourself of all of the different tools that you can use.

I would like to feel that you will use this guide as a roadmap, as a starting point of reference for your own journey into health and wellbeing and also a source of inspiration. You can look at this guide and think to yourself, 'It is possible to overcome this', 'I can do it', 'All is not lost', 'There is a way!' and use it as a springboard that propels you into making your own unique discoveries about what works for you and your recovery.

I wish you all the best.

You can do it!

Richard Forbes Steven

www.psychosisrecoveryguide.com

ACKNOWLEDGEMENTS

A huge thank you to the late Namkhai Norbu Rinpoche, without whom, I am not sure that I would have recovered enough to have written this book. To my therapist, for being a great therapist. To Elis Lubja for providing inspiration and motivation for me to get going on this project. To Julia Lawless for mentoring me, proof reading, typo checking, feedback and encouragement. To my Mum, Judith Steven, and also Amely Becker and Sean G. for checking through the text for typos, giving extensive feedback and for much valued encouragement, and support.

RESOURCES

Books

Meditation & Being Present

'Reconciliation: Healing the Inner Child'
by Thich Nhat Hahn

'The Miracle of Mindfulness: An Introduction to the Practice of Meditation'
by Thich Nhat Hahn, Vo-Dihn Mai, et al.

'Meditation in Action'
by Chogyam Trungpa

'Dzogchen: The Self Perfected State'
by Chogyal Namkhai Norbu

'The Mirror: Advice on the Presence of Awareness'
by Chogyal Namkhai Norbu

'The Power of Now'
by Eckhart Tolle

Diet & Lifestyle

'Healing With Whole Foods: Asian Traditions and Western Nutrition' by Paul Pitchford

'Birth, Life and Death' by Chogyal Namkhai Norbu

Chinese and Tibetan Medicine / Complementary Therapies

'Birth, Life and Death' by Chogyal Namkhai Norbu

'Healing from the Source: The Science and Lore of Tibetan Medicine' by Dr Yeshi Dhonden

'The Web that Has No Weaver: Understanding Chinese Medicine' by Ted Kaptchuk

'Wisdom in the Body: The Craniosacral Approach to Essential Health' by Michael Kern

'I Ching or Book of Changes' by Jung, Wilhelm and Baynes

'The Yellow Emperor's Classic of Medicine: A New Translation of the Neijing Suwen with Commentary' by Maoshing Ni

'Tibetan Buddhist Medicine and Psychiatry: The Diamond Healing' by Terry Clifford

Relationships, Communication, Sex and Intimacy

'Attached: The New Science of Adult Attachment and How It Can Help You Find - and Keep - Love' by Amir Levine and Rachel Heller

'Sex at Dawn: The Prehistoric Origins of Modern Sexuality' by Christopher Ryan and Cacilda Jetha

'How to be a 3% Man'
by Corey Wayne

'Mating in Captivity: Unlocking Erotic Intelligence'
by Esther Perel

'How to Win Friends and Influence People'
by Dale Carnegie

Sleep

'Sleep: The Myth of 8 Hours, the Power of Naps… and the New Plan to Recharge your Body and Mind'
by Nick Littlehales

'Birth, Life and Death' by Chogyal Namkhai Norbu

Yantra Yoga & Harmonious Breathing

'Yantra Yoga: The Tibetan Yoga of Movement'
by Chogyal Namkhai Norbu and Adriano Clemente

'Tibetan Yoga of Movement: The Art and Practice of Yantra Yoga'
by Chogyal Namkhai Norbu, Fabio Andrico, et al.

'Healing with Yantra Yoga: From Tibetan Medicine to the Subtle Body' by Elio Guarisco and Phuntsog Wangmo

'Breathe As You Are: Harmonious Breathing for Everyone'

by Fabio Andrico

Video

Yantra Yoga & Harmonious Breathing

The Eight Movements of Yantra Yoga
with Fabio Andrico

Tibetan Yoga of Movement: Perfect Rhythm of Life Level
I, with Fabio Andrico and Laura Evangelisti

Tibetan Yoga of Movement: Perfect Rhythm of Life Level
II, with Fabio Andrico and Laura Evangelisti

Breathe: The Perfect Harmony of Breathing
with Fabio Andrico and Yamila Diaz

◆ ◆ ◆

Web: www.psychosisrecoveryguide.com
Instagram: @psychosis_recovery_guide
Facebook: @psychosisrecoveryguide
Twitter: @psychosisguide

Printed in Great Britain
by Amazon

20919880R00120